The World Around Me
with Songs and Poetry

Shawn Jones

The World Around Me
with Songs and Poetry

Shawn Jones

Published by:

Whispering Pine Press International, Inc.
Your Northwest Book and Gift Company
507 N. Sullivan Road Suite LL-5
Spokane Valley, WA 99037-8576 USA
Phone: (509) 928-8700 | Fax: (509) 922-9949
Websites: www.whisperingpinepress.com
www.whisperingpinepressbookstore.com
Blog: www.whisperingpinepressblog.com
Email: sales@whisperingpinepress.com
SAN 253-200X
Printed in the U.S.A.

Published by Whispering Pine Press International, Inc.
507 N. Sullivan Road Suite LL-5
Spokane Valley, Washington 99037-8576 USA

Copyright © 2012 by Shawn Jones
All rights reserved.

No part of this publication may be reproduced, translated, stored in a retrieval system, or transmitted in any form by any means, including electronic, mechanical photocopying, recording, or otherwise without the prior written permission from the publisher, Whispering Pine Press International, Inc.

For sales outside the United States, please contact the Whispering Pine Press International, Inc., International Sales Department.

Manufactured in the United States of America.

Book and Cover Designed by: Artistic Book and Web Design
c/o Artistic Design Service, Inc.
507 N. Sullivan Road, Suite LL-6
Spokane Valley, WA 99037-8576 USA
www.artisticdesignservice.com

Library of Congress Control Number (LCCN): 2012900095

Jones, Shawn
    Title: The World Around Me with Songs and Poetry

    p.   cm.

ISBN: 978-1-59434-594-4   perfect bound
ISBN: 978-1-59434-595-1   E-PDF
ISBN: 978-1-59434-603-3   E-PUB
ISBN: 978-1-59434-855-6   E-PRC

First Edition: May 2012
1. Poetry   1. Title

To the world around me.

The World Around Me
with Songs and Poetry

Gift Inscription

To: _____

From: _____

Date: _____

Special Message: _____

_____

_____

_____

_____

_____

_____

It is always nice to receive a personal note to create a special memory.

Table of Contents

Title Page 1
Publisher Page 3
Copyright Page 4
Dedication 5
Gift Inscription 7
Table of Contents 9-18
Songs and Poetry:
    I've Got to Find My Brothers 21
    Little Leaf 22
    Through Her I See You 23
    Judy 24
    You're Naked Beneath Me 25
    Completely Done 26
    Shoot the Breeze 27
    Pure as Sour Cream 28
    In Midair 29
    I Wanna Slide into You 30
    Wanta Hold You Online and Off 31
    She Did It First 32
    Go Ahead Catch the Key to My Ride 33
    Seek Me Don't Hide 34-35
    I'm Sorry 36-37
    Behind a Tree 38
    So Stay 39
    Smell the Light of the Candle 40
    W-2 Me 41
    Dancing in My Car 42
    Stealing More Than the Sheets 43
    Just Untangled a Bit 44
    A Bike Biter 1 45
    Fly-by-Nighters 46
    The Final Spin 47

Kiss 'n Tale	48
Kiss the Sane Away	49
Kiss Me before You Knew Me	50-51
Love and Leave	52-53
Memoirs of Hell	54
Minutes	55
Look in the Mirror	56
Adorable	57
Feel You	58-59
Not Just Anyone	60
Time Well Spent	61
Old News	62
My Lilly Gets to Me	63
Never on the Left Side Just Closer on the Right	64-65
The Nolands	66-67
I Love Your Tone	68
He's My Man	69
Redless	70
I Try to Tell You	71
Hold On!	72-74
It's Your Loss You Toss	75
Here's the Book, I've Got the Pages	76
My Ankle Bracket Had a Hold on Me	77
Yes I May Be a Bum	78
Time of Passion	79
You Might Find Mr. Right	80-81
Tic-Tac-Toe	82
Cherry Red	83
Who Gave You Your First Step	84-85
Hey, Got a Moment	86
They're Riding My Shirttail	87
Rubbing in Your Tub	88

We've Been Smoking 89
The Heck with You 90
Wrong Keys 91
I'd Like to Know 92
Yellow Rose 93
Why Not Me 94-95
When I Was Young 96-97
Who Has a Light 98-99
Whatever 100-101
I Am Not Going to Cry 102
My Level 103
Tasting Red Lips 104
I Am Check'n 105
Liar, Liar, His Pants Are on Fire Again 106
What I Like 107
We Made It on the 4th 108-109
Dimension 110
Two Thumbs Up 111
Walking on Logs 112
Trick or Treat 113
I Was Sweet till She Got Away 114
Touching the Numbness 115
Touch My G String 116
There's No Way I Can Do 117
Sugar and Spice, Fire and Ice 118
Tell Someone Else 119
Take That Step 120
Dancing with You Online 121
Remember First Love 122-123
She's Just Too Old 124
Tag Me Alive 125
Noticing Me 126-127

My Teardrop 128-129
Hitting the 18th Mark.. 130-131
Pain from Our Knuckles 132
Mommy Even Tho 133
Morning Still...134
Do You Love Me 135
Look Me in the Eye..136
Laying in Her Bed..137
Under the Christmas Lights 138
Lost My Loose Jeans..139
Looking for Love That Floats Up..140
Eclipse..141
In a Spiderman Wheelchair 142-143
Making Peace with You 144
Saddle it Up with a Bounce 145
Last Days with My Dad 146
Just Tell Me When...147
If You Could Only Understand 148
I've Lost You...149
I'm Sorry I Hung Up...150
If You Let Him He Will Hurt You 151
I'm Not a Blond but You I Can Touch...................................... 152-153
I'm Trying to Get to Heaven..154
I'm Used to Two...155
I Just Met You 156-157
I'm Your Love, Love Pad 158
I Have No Clue, Do You 159
Free from Me 160
Fall for You..161
Help My Friend Don't Take Her...162
Strawberry Hill...163
High off Life 164

Here's to a Girl That Didn't Get It 165
Her or Me 166-167
The Days Go By 168
He Is Gone 169
He Knew a Friend 170
Getting Her Feet Dirty 171
Getting Lost While Finding Him 172
Your Life 173
You Say You Have a Fiancée 174
Forget Me Nots 175
Fingerprints on Your Pants 176
Fake It, Make It 177
I Will Never Blink 178
Every Which Way 179
Debbie 180
Crunching Down 181
Crystal Ball Inside Me 182
Warm from Your Form 183
Be Not Afraid 184
Be with You 185
Acquaintance 186-187
Parachute 188
Taking Care of His Own World 189
Call House Blues 190-192
Bounce into Your Heart 193
Battery 194
All I Did Was Wake Her Up 195
At Ease 196-197
A Gay Guy Holding My Hand 198
Receiving Is Believing 199
I Wanta Touch On 200-201
Portrait of a Teenager's Dream 202

A Blink of an Eye	203
15 Days and Loving Every Minute	204
A Blazing Sun	205
10 A.M.	206-207
Melt with You There's Nothing I Wouldn't Do	208
A Goodbye to You and I	209
Our Life Speeds by Me	210-211
In the Light of Shawn's Eyes	212
In My Empty Guitar Case	213
Don't Be a Fool Over a Stupid Guy	214
Give Me Your MySpace	215
I Used to Know	216
Skin to Skin	217
Tuck Me In	218-219
Running Down My Side	220-221
Sucking Up the Heat	222
I Know You're Such a Young Toy	223
He Said Where Is She At	224
Friendship Love	225
Dream Time Wasted	226
Grandma Trot	227
Boxers with Red, Red Kisses	228
Black Lace	229
Clinging on to the Hold That Couldn't Let Go	230-232
Is My Number Really Up	233
Want Some Damn Lovin'	234
In a Doublewide	235
On the Eastside	236
This Is the Bus for Me	237
I Wasn't Supposed To	238-239
Blue-Eyed Baby Girl	240
Fishing for My Medication	241

Shot Down	242
Why Can't I Fit In	243
Let Me Play with It Hard	244
Take the Shorts Corner	245
He Touch My Tail	246
Monogamous	247
Could There Be a Reason Why	248
2 A.M. Kiss at the Light	249
I Did It with My Dad Twice	250-251
I Did It on My Own	252
Makala, Makala	253
Up on South Hill	254
You're Lucky That	255
It's So Hard to Forgive	256
Who Was That Guy That Gave Me a Warm Hug Online	257
3 Magic Words	258
Math Piece	259
Mom in My Heart	260-261
Drip, Drip, off My Lip	262
Five Alive	263
The World Keeps on Changing	264-265
He's Not Yours	266
The Court in Our White House	267
Sexy Colors Really Matter	268
Coffee, Tea, Come Fly with Me United Airlines	269
Aloha	270
The Last Kennedy to Go	271
Twin Towers	272-273
Rolling Up onto Shore	274-275
The Wrong That Could Have Been Right	276-277
Lady Diana	278

You Promised Me a Roll and a Stone 279
Remember Michael 280
With the Glove 281
Still Ends Up Like a Virgin..282
From Top to Bottom Headed Back Up....................................283
Like Thunder 284
Carrying under the Wood Now on a Log 285
Saxophone Became Sexy Cell Phone..286
Billy Ray 287
She's My Time after Time..288
Going through Hell...289
His Eyes Are on His Sunglasses..290
My Son Named Beau 291
Thinks He's a Singing Rancher 292
Just Let Me...293
My Oldest Listens to Him 294
What I Can Show You...295
Yes, I'm Going... 296-297
Now My Son Can 298
Whoopi Goldberg...299
Rosie O'Donnell 300
Andrew and Fergie 301
Betty Boop 302
She Dances on In 303
Flying Colors..304
The Empty Cart 305
Farrah...306
Where Is Indiana Jones..307
Oprah 308
Humpty Became Dummy 309
Dorothy and Tin Man...310
I'm the Gingerbread Woman 311

Drake and Josh and Sister Megan	312
He Started Out Dumb and Stupid	313
I Had a Beach McIntyre Too	314-315
So Young	316
Beau of Our Lives	317
First Her Son, Now Her	318
Spokaneless	319
Back to the Future Hits the Present	320-321
Believe in Your Heart	322-325
Water on the Rocks	326
McDonald's Make a McTurkey	327
Senior Citizen Jeopardy	328
Wheel of Text	329
The Shot That Takes Care of You	330
Shriners	331
This Is the Place Odyssey	332
Thank God for Fridays	333
Deliver My Taste	334
Staples Is the Place	335
Walker	336
I Bought My First Boots at Walmart	337
So Bee ... My Honey	338
Closest Thing Being over New York	339
Wells Fargo	340
State Farm	341
Crest is My Main Squeeze	342
The Christmas Cats Tales	343
The Almighty Dollar	344
Not As Dumb As I Am Blonde	345
Walgreens Lasts Longer	346
Speed Dating with a Chocolate Kiss	347
Are You Here	348-349

- I Want to Be under Your Purple Rain 350-352
- My Blanket of Balloons 353
- Crumbs of Thought, Whole Bread Instead 354
- What's Your Best Score? 355
- Want a Drink, No Just a Coke 356
- Talk Never Said a Word 357
- Call in the Next 10 Minutes, It's Free 358
- Ginger Man 359
- Where's Mr. Winky 360
- Tic-Tac, I Can Be Very Friendly 361
- Going Bankrupt and Still Paying the Bill 362
- Chocolate 363
- Just Hand Over the Chocolate 364
- The Y M C A 365
- What Am I Talking About 366
- Guys Get Water on the Rocks 367
- Gold Woman 368
- Whispering into Your Hearts 369
- Holidays 370

Design & Typeset Page 371
Alphabetical Index by Title 372-381
Alphabetical Index by First Line 382-393
Reader Feedback Form 394
Order Form 395
About the Author 396

Songs and Poetry

I'VE GOT TO FIND MY BROTHERS

I've got to find my brothers
I feel my life won't be complete
Until I meet my birth mother
I can hardly eat

Traveled back to the place I was born
I longed for this day
Only to be torn
My mother had passed away

Read the next of kin
Call him up and past begin
I found my brothers
Fill my heart with joy
Picture of my mother
With all the boys

Learned about my father
And the Shorts corner
A whole new family to meet
Now my life is complete

Now I have my brothers
And memories of my mother and father

June 11, 2008

LITTLE LEAF

Little leaf changing in the sun
While you and I running around having fun
Since I met you, I don't want plans
Just take my hand

No more trigs in my world
Tell me are you my girl
Come on babe run free
Just let us be

Roll down the hill without a care
Into each other's arms without a fear
Leaving the world behind
Just you and me in the middle of time

Little leaf changing in the sun
While you and I running around having fun
Since I met you I don't want plans
Just take my hand

Feel the sun on your face
This is our place
Now I am at peace
With myself and the human race

No more trigs in my world
Tell me are you my girl

THROUGH HER I SEE YOU

Seeing you again
After all these years
Wonder deep inside while
Touching you with tears

What I can't say to him
You hold me and listen in
I can stand on my own two feet
Feel her heart beat

All the pain I went through
You were right there too
Even though we belong to someone else
I have you to myself

Now she is born and you'll
Be back with her
And me with him just like before
Through her I see you
Dancing around the room
I watch our baby bloom

Hold on never to let her go
Hoping to see her dad so

JUDY

If I could I'd take you back
Take you back
I would take you to a place of the unknown
A place that is filled with love
A place you never ever heard of

I would show you the beauty
Promise you roses Judy
If I could take you back
You'd be next to me
I'd show you how life should be

While I wander through the park
I am walking by the water
Thoughts of you in the dark
I remember my little daughter
As I look at my reflection I see you
From the light of the sun it's true

I will take you to the park
Hold your hand as we walk
And show you my wandering pains
As we talk about our new land

I will show you my beauty
Promise you roses Judy
As I hold your hand
Show my wonderland
And we will be together once again
As we are with each other until the end

YOU'RE NAKED BENEATH ME

You're naked beneath me
I could hear all the noises

I could feel your skin
So
Even your heartbeat
But we are apart

So what I am trying
To say I want you
Here
I want you beneath
Me again
Are you here?

You're so beautiful
With your hair back
I look into your
Eyes I know you
Don't want to go
Your toes are rubbing me

You're naked beneath
Me
Please let it be
I miss you
And love you
I miss you
And love you
Your toes are rubbing me

COMPLETELY DONE

Remember the night
In your eyes shining light
I had to choose between the three of you
God that was hard to do

One so very gentle
He was an angel
I wasn't sure why
Yet he was very shy

One of the others
Seemed so together
He had this smile
That made me go wild

The last one I was not sure of
We were pretending to be in love
He was so understanding and sweet
He would be so hard to beat

We first had our life set
Just a little acted until we met
You and I, the others, somehow choose
You and I would lose

I felt I should cling
To the other one I would lean
But the gentle one
Love felt so completely done

SHOOT THE BREEZE

Okay this is me earth
You are all the way over here
In the middle we came together
Just for a short time not forever

Is there a speeding light
Don't push it tonight
What are you thinking
My heart is breaking
I try so hard, I didn't get far

Learning all I can about you
Still not getting through
Yet laughing till dawn
Wanting so deeply to belong

Letting yourself feel sensible
You are so impossible
Shot the breeze
You and me

This is earth
You are here, way over here
Let it go honey
It wasn't that funny
Laughing till dawn
Thanks so much Shawn

PURE AS SOUR CREAM

Pure as sour cream
My life is just a dream
So many things
My eyes fill and beam

Tasting the daisy
Saying love me, love me not
I just want to tie the knot
But he's too lazy
Making more than dip fine
I want his lips to sip mine
Why he tries to split
I feel the end of the pit
As he touches my tit

Pure as sour cream
My life is just a dream
So I sit in a bowl
Feel cold and low
Still he takes a bite
Yet not of me
Just sour cream dip so lite
As I pull on his daisy
Saying love me, love me not

December 22, 2008

IN MIDAIR

Needed someone to hold me in midair
Feeling the breeze down there
Let's step into the basket
Float away over the ocean
The flame on our faces
As our mind races

See the world in the wind
No longer we can pretend
Wind blowing in my hair
Feeling the breeze again down there
Holding each other close not to bend over
Into the blue sky seeing the mountains fly over
Up, up, in the clouds so high
Him in shaking the basket again
All in midair
Feeling the love down there
Never touching the ground
In a hot air balloon floating around
In midair

Feeling the breeze down there
You and I without a care
My love will always be here
Promise you the world of my heart
Hoping never to fall apart
Landing in a new start

October 2, 2008

I WANNA SLIDE INTO YOU

I wanna slide into you
Put the ring through your tongue
As I touch the dirty blonde
With every breath I feel
Your thoughts I will steal

Cold like half naked
I cover you with my blanket
Reaching the pinkest
Into your heart
With every part

As each sound came out
Your moan is my groan
Oohhh, oohhh, oohh

Now our love is real
And you are my thrill
As we grow, uh ohhh
Making my way down low

I wanna slide into you
Put the ring through your tongue
And believe in you and me
Making us free
Just love me

To Nick and Katie
December 6, 2009

WANTA HOLD YOU ONLINE AND OFF

Are you seeking or just peeking
Lost 62 lbs., 43, DWF mother
Seeking that blue-collar male 30 to 45
Let's barbeque, throw Frisbee,
Wet in the pool
Run in the sand
Dance in the moonlight
Take a chance on me ...
Hold on to me ...
Nonsmoker, water on the rocks,
Don't do drugs, get high off life
Up for the beat in the heat
So let's seek and do more than peek
Let's meet and rub feet

SHE DID IT FIRST

You told me all about her
Now I'm your new lover
She did it to you first
Now you are at your worst

Bring in your 2-year-old son
Not wanting to let go
Taking care of the both of you
While he missed his momma so

She came to the door
Here's your son, but I have him
You don't want her anymore
The lights draw dim

Then I felt a baby inside
You still married
It's just not right
I close my eyes
Ending it that night
I can't have you
What do I do

GO AHEAD CATCH
THE KEY TO MY RIDE

Go ahead catch a ride on me
Feed my mind when you're with theirs
Become one with our wings
Catch a ride any size, drop on by

Like a kite you're in my wind
Go ahead drop a line, put on that key
Become that tree as we dangle in the sky
Scarce free of electricity

Go ahead catch a ride on me
See the light as the rain hits
You and I drop on by feeling my wind
As the saddle touches our skin

Go ahead catch the key to my ride
You and I now became the key
To electricity

By Savannah Jones
December 3, 2008

SEEK ME DON'T HIDE

Seek me don't hide
Find me on the line
Don't stop and think
Just count out of order and be mine

Odey ox free, you found me
928 now you're closer to my ear
Feeling your breath I can hear
Close your eyes
I'm here with a picture inside
Down deep I am not going to hide
Closing your eyes once again
Now I'm your friend
As you spell your e-mail order
On your phone, we are not alone

Hiding go seek
Now you can peek
So I can sneak
But you can't cheat
Because I'm in heat

Get hard and off your feet
Odey ox free you found me
Don't let me be free
I don't want to sleep around
With you I just wanta get down
Count, baby count out of order
Find me, find me on line
Soon you will fall
On the ground laughing with a smile
Just be here for awhile
Hiding go seek, you've peeked
Inside me, behind a line

Now I'm not odey ox free
Find me, find me now I can be

I'M SORRY

I don't want you to
Leave me hanging
I know but I can't go
I've got so much to do you know
Yet I'm calling you

It only takes a day
To get here you pay
Getting on a plane
You are driving me insane

I'm sorry
I'm so sorry
Loving you makes
Me worry
I have a girl
But I don't know if
She's mine
I touch you in my dreams
And mind

My friends tell me to
But I can't leave my family behind
With you on line
Knowing I want you to
Be mine

I'm sorry
I'm so sorry
Loving you makes
Me worry

But I don't want to be that
Stupid guy
In your eye
Just Mr. Right
So sorry tonight
Call me again and be the light

I'm sorry
I'm so sorry

To John 44
December 11, 2009

BEHIND A TREE

She took me behind a tree
And she told me
How she felt then she took my hand
And said, you're my man

Then she touched me like this
And she gave me a kiss
I thought it was cool
Yet I felt like a fool

He has always been shy
But a special guy
To me can't you see
Behind a tree

To Kinshasa
July 29, 2008

SO STAY

I looked at your picture today
I dialed your number to hear you
But I just couldn't get through

You seem so far away
I couldn't wait three whole days
Your lips make me say
I want you close so stay

Holding my hand
Telling me again and again
That we will never end
You seem to understand

You are here
I will always care
Staring into your eyes
For now it's you and I

So hold me in your arms
For I am no longer sure
That together we will be
Just you and me

Show me that you really care
Tell me that you're willing to share
The closeness of us as one
For our life must go on until done
So why don't you stay
So stay
Don't go today
So stay

SMELL THE LIGHT OF THE CANDLE

Here I am, there you are
Touch as we fall
Emotion giving you my all
Smell the light of the candle
Turn the handle, repeat the song

Touching you feels so right not wrong, not wrong
Take the breath, feel your heart
Sliding down making a new start
Run your hands through my hair
The moment is right there, right there, right there

Smell the light of the candle
Grip that handle
Holding on tight
Come on baby doll

Oh Honey, come on just say yes
On through the night, slow not fast
Put them on my hips
Just like this
Hold us to sleep
The candle go out
Not even a pout

W-2 ME

I'm laying on a smooth hard desk
Under all these papers
I'm trying to find someone to file
Checking out my dotted line for miles

Come on W-2 me
Let the papers fly free
Taxes run me down
Is it you I've found
In my brown hair
Red ink lips I cross there
The money I get back is the pits
But I'm not going to have a fit
Big 44 – W-2 hits those eyes
Hoping your numbers don't lie

That hardly green machine
File, file me but not too mean
Do I need to pay extra
To get the check in faster
W-2 me until my bills are free
Now get me out from under these papers
And bend me over with one number
Not some line, I'm fine
W-2 me like you're mine

March 6, 2009

DANCING IN MY CAR

Now I slow down
And back up
But my lights are still on

Oh, I forgot to turn
Them off
At least I have on one signal
It's you my left
That's right dear
Oh, boy
Are you giving me
The right-of-way
Or just passing me by

No I already did
Don't you know me kid

Dancing in my car
Slow but I can get far
I'll find you wherever you are

Try not to dare
I want to go bare
I just want you to care

STEALING MORE THAN THE SHEETS

Calling me up
Saying you're too drunk
You need a ride
I told a lie

You are up
You need more than a cup
Feel all sad and blue
Hold me you know what to do

Stealing more than the sheets
We just had to meet
Rubbing your feet
I can feel the warm heat

Doing the twist and turn
Letting the others get burned
Loving each other until noon
Check out too soon

Stealing more than the sheets
Rush back to repeat
Again we meet
I can still feel the warm heat

JUST UNTANGLED A BIT

You know I want to belong
I don't know how strong
This love could carry on
But I am willing to stay
Taking it day by day

You may use me
Or try to confuse me
But I know my love
Is what I am thinking of
It may be very long
But I can't wait here strong

You've got to understand
That I am here to give you a hand
Just untangled a bit
We can make this love a hit

Just hold yourself close to me
Then you will soon see
My love is very much you
My love is very much true

So just untangled a bit
Hold me and please don't forget
Babe my love this is it
You and I are a hit

Now we are alone
A quiet at home
Darkness of fire and candles
I touch your hair no more tangles

Just untangled a bit
And we can make this love a hit

A BIKE BITER 1

My baby is one horny rider
he gets on and my wheels spin
as he holds on to me again
they call him the bike biter
but he's no fighter
just my easy rider

With his hair tied back
silk leather touches my black
the wind hits our glass helmet
as he squeezes my ass
he rides around my curves
as I turn left and sever

On the dirt roads we go
in the street we meet saying no
holing on down
low as the ground

My baby is one horny rider
he gets on and my wheels spin
kick up that stick run so smooth
you know I'm in the mood
they call him the bike biter
but he's no fighter
just my easy rider

March 5, 2009

FLY-BY-NIGHTERS

These are the men
That come and go
Into my life
They have no plans
Just wanted desires
A fantasy in the wind
You talk sexy on the phone
Hoping not to be alone
Meeting them to hold their hand
Feeling the heartbeat in their pants
Letting them touch each part of your skin
Not wanting every moment to end
But they realize you're not just a show
Seeing what's around them they get up and go
Fly-by-nighters
Somehow I remember their face, name
Some have wives, children, and girlfriends
But I was once their fly-over-nighters
They were once my lover no
They are fly-by-nighters
Run off into the night
Once a rider now a hider

January 14, 2009

THE FINAL SPIN

Once again
Attention still mounting
Feeling each word
On the phone
Telling you're
So alone
The Final Spin
I am holding on
Trying to win
Racing through my body
Wanting a part of you
The Final Spin
Together in the end
Your heart your soul
No more on the edge
The blues left when
I touched you
At least I had thought
Then came The Final Spin
Coming back I showed you
Looking the other way
You kissed me anyways
My heart began to spin
Now we are together again

January 14, 2009

KISS 'N TALE

Here I sit dressed in nothing but yellow
Went upstairs to kiss a fellow
Came back down with a
Snake in my ass
It felt so good that he made a pass
I went back upstairs again
Hoping it would last
Now I'm kissing ass
Oh what a blast
Hey baby give me your ass
As we kiss 'n tale
Where is my male
I'm here in there
No one wants to come anymore
It didn't hurt before
They just want to screw
I'm through with you
No more kiss 'n tale

Kissing Ass
October 10, 2008

KISS THE SANE AWAY

Kiss the pain
Kiss the sane away
I need you to stay
Away from me

I can't handle this anymore
Let me go, let me go
I just don't need you
I need a clear sky
Not clouds in my way

Bring in the sun
What happened to the love
I can't stand this mud
I need the wind I can get
I don't need this pain yet

Kiss the pain
Kiss the sane away
Like a bird, set me free
I need you to stay
Away from me

KISS ME BEFORE YOU KNEW ME

Those girls are too young
I may be old but I still
Can get it on
Kiss me before you knew me
Walking away I'm still free
You came back with your number
But I like them young too, saying whatever

You trying too hard to be on stage
Take a look at your age
Why I play and not touch
Maybe a little but not so much
You say I'm beautiful you fool
I know you tell all the girls
Wishing your touch may rule
I'm just in another world

We both somehow belong
Just hold on tight and strong
Have that last drink
Giving her time to think
She said goodbye one more time
You tried to use a line

Kiss me before you knew me
Walking away I'm still free
I caught you looking again
As I was touching him
You say I want to be with you
But I've only been with a few
My heart is torn blue
Kiss me before you knew

Kiss me before you knew me
Walking away I'm still free

February 28, 2009

LOVE AND LEAVE

Holding him tightly
Kissing him lightly
He said what's that for
I said I don't want it like this anymore
He said I don't quite understand
I thought I was the only man

A tear down from my eye
As I said the last words goodbye
He was a man who would love and leave
Love and leave
I should of took back my keys
But somehow I felt he would stay
I didn't want him to go away

Every time he came back
It would last a little while then he
Would be on his track
I wish I knew why
How come he never said goodbye
Love and leave

The way he said I'll hold on to these
Love and leave
Baby I'll be back soon
Someday half past noon

Now I had my mind
Made up I wasn't going to wait this time
You see I had to make it
I had to learn to take it

Love and leave
Was not going to be for me
When he came back I was on my track

Holding him tightly kissing him lightly
With a tear from my eye saying goodbye
But I still have the key
Holding on to them after all these years
I wonder as I open the door, is it him
I could not believe the tears

Love and leave
Never let go of these
He never did, he never did

MEMOIRS OF HELL

Memoirs of hell
Do you remember how we fell
Memoirs of you and I
We fell in love, why
Did it end this way
I am sorry to say

Memoirs of hell
God I wish I could tell
You goodbye
After all those lies

Memoirs of hell
Why didn't you tell
Me everything
Now my feelings
Have gone to hell
Why didn't you tell

I still love you so
Even though I already know
The truth about you
Why did you lie, what did I do

Memoirs of hell
Now on my own till
The feelings are gone
I will be still inside
I have learned to go through the night
I can go on without you, it's all right

MINUTES

The minutes may pass by
As we look up at the sky
The memories of you and I
As I close my eyes
It seems to hold on and on
With your life, can't go wrong

The beauty of the sunlight
And you here by my side
I am holding on so tight
Each time seems to be the last night

There are times I feel down and out
There are times when there is no doubt
That I still care for you
The memories I want to hold on to

The minutes are now gone of you
There is nothing I can do
There is no one else but you
That I really want to hold on to

For life is no longer without you
For your love is no longer true
There is no other person but you for me
I love you, can't you really see

LOOK IN THE MIRROR

Look in the mirror
What do you see
A face of a man
But what could he be

I see eyes
With a picture inside
Life I see each day
But is he this way

I look at the trees
But when will he be free
In the mirror I see him
I wonder if he is like them

The picture in his eyes
Makes me want to know why
He wants to fly
Up way up into the sky
Time after time he wonders
What he should do if there is thunder
The world is him on wings
Under him life and other things
Still is as free
Even when he is high above the trees
Is he really free

Look in the mirror
A face of a man
I still wonder if he understands
What's out there
And does he care what's going on here

ADORABLE

I'm so comfortable
yet reasonably affordable
they say I'm lovable
even adorable

You could easily lose your mind
dancing and laughing all the time
it may be just a mist
but you're on my list

As I hold on to your body like this
making you tell me more than once
I'll still feel you twice

This is so right
you can have me tonight
I'm so comfortable
yet reasonably affordable
they say I'm lovable
even adorable

October 3, 2009

FEEL YOU

I used to feel you in the dark
Now it's a lost heart
Miles and miles apart
Hoping you didn't forget
But now you forgot
Where did we start
Trying so hard to get
You back into my heart

What did I used to see
You holding on to me
My eyes open as you touch
Feeling you inside so much
What happened to us
Warmth hit cold as we got old
The view was still you
Even though I thought it was through
How can I leave you

Wanting to talk about it like this
Trying to remember those lips
Come back with that kiss
That I missed

I used to feel you in the dark
Now it's a lost heart
Miles and miles apart
Now it's a lost heart
Hoping you didn't forget
But now you forgot
Where did we start
Trying so hard to get
You back into my heart

Feel you in the dark
Now it's a lost heart
Miles and miles apart

October 3, 2009

NOT JUST ANYONE

I need someone
Not just anyone
But somebody
Not just anybody
To love me

My heart reaches out
Who are you all about
Tears in my eyes
Just want to hold you tonight
But I don't know what's so right
Are you what's so right

I love you on the east side
Never the north side
Sometimes I go over to the south side
Only to find you back on the west side

I need someone
Not just anyone
But somebody
Not just anybody
To love me
I need you

To Jerry

TIME WELL SPENT

Time well spent
When you were there to invent
Knowing your mind and body
Every hour was more than an hour
Dressing up for your girl
Thinking she's the world

Calling and saying the right words
Opening up the door for more
Pulling out a chair without a care
Picnic in the park
Dancing till dark
Whatever happened to
Strawberry and whipped cream
You're only in my dreams

Telling secrets till dawn
Flowers given once again
Holding hands, where is my man
Kissing me softly again and again

June 29, 2009

OLD NEWS

You say I'm old news
And there's nothing I can do
Why is it up to her not you
Now we both lose
Since you met her I'm not in
The group
No longer your bowl of soup
We used to do it all
Laughing in your car

Now you pass me by
But I can still see it in your eyes
When you pull me aside
And say I'll meet you later, kissing me bye
Don't tell me, don't tell me
I'm old news
When you're holding on to me too
I'm not secondhand
You used to be my man

I don't care if the new girl talks
My hand is still in yours while we walk
Hiding behind the door
Meeting in the same place as before
Don't tell me that anymore
I'm old news
I used to be new
When you still kissed me like that
Stop keeping my number under your hat

I'm not old news

September 29, 2009

MY LILLY GETS TO ME

She's so free at three
It's just her and me
My others are grown
With her I'm not alone

I leave her at preschool
So she can have fun and rule
As I work through the day
I think of her in every way

She has so much to say
As I work hard making my pay
I have my last lucky charm
Running into my arms

My Lilly gets to me
Doing it in circles just like me
I see her dreams come true
With the colors she will use

She is so free at three
Looking up at me
Dancing as we sing
It's our thing

My Lilly gets to me
She's the joy of my others
Inside her eyes
I love being a mother
Kicking her feet up high

She really gets to me

September 23, 2009

NEVER ON THE LEFT SIDE
JUST CLOSER ON THE RIGHT

He made sure of my name
Moving closer just the same
Through the night
Through the night

Numbers passed through phones
No longer dancing alone
I somehow knew
The feeling of you

He called me when I returned home
I put his name in my phone
Meeting again, just talking to him
Touching more than our hands
Where was my heart going to land

Soft and smooth yet so alive
He was interested in my insides
That our love began to survive
I could see more in his eyes

Never on the left side
Just closer on the right
I felt your heartbeat through the night
In the heat it felt so tight
With the fan blowing up on us
The wind touching my chest
I felt a drip
Ice from your lips

Never on the left side
Just closer on the right
You ended, dropping me in tears
The next night I was in fears
You got what you wanted, a little loving
Now you're no longer holding

THE NOLANDS

Breeze blowing through my hair
I am wishing you were there
Walking down the hill
I notice everything was still
I touch the grass
And remember the past
We thought it would last
But that was the past
At the end of the hill
I stop completely still
And everything came alive
I wish you would arrive

I felt then that life was gone
I was in a place I called home
I was very much alone
Then I begin to walk on my own
Seeing things I never saw
Being with it all
Walking through the trees
I felt so happy, so free
A world of peace
A world of just me

I could do anything, even out loud sing
The day was soon going away
The night started right away
A moon surrounded with stars
I know where you are
I made it up the hill
I wanted that one more thrill
Looking around
But did not hear a sound
Felt I was very wrong and turn to see you
Gone but you were there to be found
I stared, couldn't believe you were here
Thank you for believing in me
Thank you for letting me be free
Just to have a little space
To find my own special place

I LOVE YOUR TONE

I love your tone
Just a voice on the phone
Can't wait to hear each sound
Every word can't bring me down

So soft and tender
I want so much to surrender
Give me the right directions to you
The rest I know what to do

Letting down my guard
Running out into the back yard
Feeling the green grass
All you had to do was ask

I love your tone
Just a voice on the phone
Can't wait to hear each sound
Falling with my feet on the ground

HE'S MY MAN

Look at him kissing him
They maybe feel that touch
Of love they needed in a man
Now they have in each other
And love again

He's my man
Look at him kiss him
They feel that touch
Each one wanted so much
They just couldn't find it
In a girlfriend

He's my man
Look at him kiss him
Giving each other
Someone to hold on to
Doing it as they text
I love you …

To Ben, Kyle's boyfriend
December 5, 2008

REDLESS

I don't wanta wear red
I am crying instead
All I do for you
Sends me back to
Being blue

Dancing in my living room
Let's dance on the floor
Where are the roses at my front door
I just want what I had before
Someone loving me more and more

I am now putting on my red
Trying to find him again
Going out, seeing couples
Looking for someone single
Is he here, is he here for me
I can't see it yet in his eyes

Dancing in my arms tonight
Hoping love is in the moonlight
I'm also inside, his lips touch mine
I'm now once again redless
Touching him I am no longer heartless
Go ahead take off my red I've got love
Next to me in bed
Take off my red
Redless

To Jerry

I TRY TO TELL YOU

Here I sit with my old guitar
I try to tell you with a song
'Cause in words
It comes out wrong

So I sit here with my guitar
Trying to tell you in a song
How I feel without a mar
So it can't be wrong

Here I am thinking about you
Wondering if it'll ever come true
I love you
Can't you see
What you are to me

Here I sit with my old guitar
I try to tell you in words
How I feel
But they just come
Out all so wrong

When you look into my eyes
I feel that there is no end
But you tell me it's all over
You said goodbye too soon

So I sit here with my old guitar
Try to tell you in a song
But the words still come out all wrong

HOLD ON!

It hurts so much
Just one little touch
Then they want everything
They feel like they're king

When their arms are around you
You feel there's nothing you can do
Hold on tight
You want it to be so right

Then the day comes
When he wants more than some
He holds on to you
Then what he heard isn't true
It's not the real love
That he'd been waiting for
You don't want what he's thinking of
He starts to close the door

You stare into his eyes
He waits for your surprise
A tear comes down
Love you though you found
Somehow he heard you've been around
Now he thinks you let him down

It hurts so much
Just one little touch
Then they want everything
They feel like they're king

He feels different now
He don't understand how
He could go wrong
He wait for you so long
Somehow he felt so strong

Looks at you for the last time
He feels that last line
Wonder what's going through your head

You wish you were dead
Who led him on
You told him it was all wrong

Now he walks outside
Somehow you couldn't sleep that night
It hurts so much
Just after that touch
You thought love was found
To bed you both were let down
In the end you must go on
No matter what goes wrong
Hold on!

That little touch
Wanted hurt so much
When you find him
It will be hard to forget about them

Soon that man will come
He might want more than some
But he will find love in you
Then you'll know what to do
You will know who to hold on to
Your dreams will come true

It hurts so much
Just after that first touch
You know you must go on
Whatever went wrong
It will soon be long gone

Hold on, hold on
You will find your love
The man that you'll think of
Just hold on, don't stop because of them
You will really find real love, it's with him

Hold on, hold on!!!

IT'S YOUR LOSS YOU TOSS

I spend everything on you
To make a family come true
But there was nothing I could do
My heart was broken too

You let me go for something
I didn't mean to do
It's your loss you toss
Now it's a lost cause

I'm sanitizing my hands and
Washing you away
Now I am clean again
And I have a new friend

It's your loss you toss
But his heart still comes alive
As you toss my heart by
With our children cry
Our new love survive

It's your loss you toss
Now you are paying the cost

November 28, 2008

HERE'S THE BOOK, I'VE GOT THE PAGES

Here is the book of our love
The nights and days we share of
But I let you go wander the sheets
While I wrote the things we did
Opening to keep our pages alive
Every word means to me
But you wanted to be free
I tried to be you with the others
But I just wanted a lover

Here's the book
I've got the pages
While you're in someone else's sheets
I have the memories
As you run wild
We still love you
Say goodbye to our
Chapters
We have reached the end
I'm closing the book on you
Thank you for our love we had
I will open the sheets
One day again I will see new pages
Come alive
But will my heart survive
As I pick up the pen and write again
Now I met someone new and I'm
Listening to his lines
Sentence becomes pages again

MY ANKLE BRACKET HAD A HOLD ON ME

I saw it in a store
Then put it on and scored
It was just like leather
But even better

Friends would ask
I let them touch
Saying you can't, no
One day I just let go

My ankle bracket
Had a hold on me
As I walked free
Into his eyes
Now he's surprised
And I am realized

One move of my ankle
He came a looking
And soon he was asking
Now we are dating

My ankle bracket
Had a hold on me
As I walked free
Now he's holding me
And I'm happy

March 6, 2009

YES I MAY BE A BUM

Yes I may be a bum
I might have more than some
Wandering the streets
Walking up to cars for some
Hoping it's you I might meet
Me on my own two feet
Can you spare more than a dime
And a little peace of mind
As I waste all my time
On little money and wine

Yes I may be a bum
But now I got some rum
And she on wheels with Tums
Taking me more for a ride
As she keep me in line I don't hide

I used to be a lost soul
With a beard and old
Now I am all cleaned up with a cup
Hot and warm to the touch
She give me so much
I still walk the streets
Hoping it's you I might meet
With my own two feet, yes I was a bum
But I still want some

TIME OF PASSION

Time of passion
You got me at the edge of time
Walking down the hall seeing you there
But I know you don't want to care
Do you really want to be near

Time of passion
Chris, Chris, Chris
Life without you
Is so very hard to do

Memories of what we had
It wasn't all that bad
Life of your passion

Waiting so long
Our love still strong
Time of passion
Why did everything go so wrong

This is my turn
Let us have love to burn
On and on passion
Why not have some action

Time of passion
You got me on the edge of time
Walking down the hall, see you there
Come on, say you want to care
God I want to have you here
Say it, say it, wanting you near

Time of passion
Chris, Chris, Chris

YOU MIGHT FIND MR. RIGHT

Years finding Mr. Right
I started my own business
Tried to be pleasant, kind and attractive
I decide to help others find their mate
So I set out and picked a place

We did barbecue and potlucks
Dances and games
Everybody was meeting everybody
But the best part was speed dating

It took a bunch of questions and three minutes
Getting to know one another
Before the night was over you picked some numbers
If you got a match by the next night
You might find Mr. Right

You go out on these dates
Try hard not to rate
After all this time
I finally found him
The lights are dim
As he said the words I'd been waiting for
I put out my hand and said yes, again and again

I can't believe it, I'm going to be engaged
After all this time, look for Mr. Right
It was just the right night and light
This was my last pager

You might find Mr. Right
Try speed dating tonight
This was my last pager

You might find Mr. Right
Try speed dating tonight
Questions, three minutes and a match
And you've got your catch

TIC-TAC-TOE

I don't play tic-tac-toe anymore
I'm just into the Xs you score
I once was a square
Full of circles in my hair
But now I compare
And draw a line
Through every X of mine
So are you ready to cross the line

I'm worth the right price
Soon there be rice
Three for three cross with me
I'm still circling with my hair
But I'm not going to X you out
Even after you cross that line
And leave me behind

Let's take the time
Not play that game shine
I'm hoping you're the last X of mine
With more circles in my hair
So are you ready to cross that line

I don't play tic-tac-toe anymore
I'm just into the Xs, you score
I once was a square
Full of circles in my hair
But now I compare
Through every X of mine
So are you ready to cross the line

March 3, 2009

CHERRY RED

Here I am in my cherry red
4-by-4 ready to pick U up
Now don't be surprise I can use a stick
Just get in and look into my eyes
Feel the leather seats, turn up the radio
Let's ride through the heat
I have a flat, you can lay in back
Go ahead and hold me close
As I put my foot on the gas
And away we go, I can drive the rain and the snow
Just like you dear. I can slide right on ice
With you I am in paradise
Free loving you and you loving me
I'll pick U up in my cherry red 4-by-4 again and again
Touch you, feel the speed, driving into the moonlight

Running my hand through the weeds, wind in my hair
Seeing the stars way up there
You and me in my cherry red, I'll pick U up in my truck
Over mountains, bring home the mud
Sitting by the ocean, sand on the rims
Whatever we did you were the only one
In my flat-back bed, I'll pick U up in my cherry red
I'll pick U up in my cherry red, get in my 4-by-4
I'll pick U up in my pickup truck

November 18, 2008

WHO GAVE YOU YOUR FIRST STEP

I met this guy who said you need a map
He shows me the red line and points at the signs
He would say you're going the wrong way
Yet I always found him
I would tell him to name the place
He would just space

He said you keep this map
I still don't know how to use it
I found my way
Yes I do U-turns
And stop and slow down

I told my mom he does get it
She said they never really get it
Or they would settle down and keep it
We all have taken that first step
No matter if someone dies or gets lost
They pay that at all cost

I went back to that man
Asked him, who gave you your first step
He said, I don't know
Then I'll give you your first step
And watch us grow

Men spend years making it big
But we buy it and bring it home and let our kids try it
My daughter said I got it
My son takes it apart
My other plays with it until he knows it by heart
Our love makes us big
All we have is a chance to show it
So don't just spend it
And wonder where it went
Save it for later when you can really spend it

November 24, 2008

HEY, GOT A MOMENT

Got a moment
I got a minute
It might take hours
But I'm only on here for an hour
I'm usually not the style
You could pop in for awhile

Are you going to take that long
Hurry up
Are you already gone
That's okay I'll just catch up with you later
Setting her with an extra platter

You can call me back
When you get back
But I don't want to wait too long
Yet I always come back to where I belong

Hoping that you've got a moment so we can get it on
Our relationship is going so strong
Now you take your time while I hurry
It along

I just love to play with you, player
Do you remember where I'm at
I got your message today
And I'm still your kitty cat
I made it back, let's play

THEY'RE RIDING MY SHIRTTAIL

They're riding my shirttail
And barking in my ear
Stop your words, I can hear
Give it time to lose my mind
Let's step off each step
Before we wept
I accept what I kept

I can hear the hurt
Craving again for the dessert
Trying to put it aside
And you back at my side

I love our children too much to hide
And I know we both have lied
Closing my eyes again and again
Saying she's doing it again, damn

February 16, 2009

RUBBING IN YOUR TUB

Rubbing in your tub
Bubbles here and there
You laugh as some touch my hair
In my ear you pucker and blow
As our love begins to flow
Holding my foot, kissing my toes
As the water goes and goes

Soft candles dim the room
Sweet smell fills the air
A spark in your eyes
Splashing water as you go under
So warm making love
Their music on
Water hits the floor
You wanting more
You bring out the rubber ducky
Oh so much love
Rubbing in your tub
I'm in love a dove

To the Boys
October 14, 2008

WE'VE BEEN SMOKING

I used to not care for smokers
But now we've been smoking
I met him in a bar
He went outside to have a smoke

I asked him to dance
Watching his tight pants
I never smelled smoke on him
Came close to touching them

He's always drunk coffee and said he was hot
He really moved on the floor
I seem to want more
He would say, show me what you've got

We would go real low
Dancing fast or slow
I used to hate the smell
Now I say, oh well

We've been smoking
And he hasn't been choking
Laughing and talking again
Dancing until it ends

October 22, 2008

THE HECK WITH YOU

The heck with you
I'm going to let down my hair
In neutral any tire to spare
With a string wheel of parts
The sound of my engine in drive
While you back up without a care
I'm easy you're mine
With every piece I'm checking inside

Touch the grease's feel
As you put in your heel
I know you'll be back
Putting it up higher
Just to check the out liner
There's nothing really
Wrong with your car
You want go that far

The heck with you
I'm going to let down my hair
Now yours is tuned up
But I'm still here with the hood up
One day I'm going to steal your heart
As you drive away with every last part

The heck with you
I'm going to let down my hair
And give you another tune-up
Hoping your engine doesn't stop
I'm going steal your heart
As you drive away with every last part

March 4, 2009

WRONG KEYS

Are these the wrong keys
Or the wrong place I am in
Always try to find them when
I fall for you
I must get up and go
But those keys run and hide
Each time we touch

Closing my eyes with you
In my arms, feel so good
I want to stay never to part
Your number is in my heart
My keys are to your door
Let me back inside
I feel so cold and alone
Without you and my keys
To your heart and door

I'D LIKE TO KNOW

I look into your eyes
I wonder why you lied
Feeling your face
I seem out of place

I wait for the true
I just wait for you
Why did you lie to me
Why didn't you let her be

I've done everything for you
And what did you do
She had to walk in
You had to see her again

Now you are holding me tight
Whispering sweet things in my ear
But I feel this is the last night
Tell me the truth my dear

For I still care for you
No matter what you may do
I'd just like to know
The reason before I go

I will care for you always
I will remember those days
Before I go, truth I want to know
Before I go, let me know right now
I'd like to know
Before I close the door and go

YELLOW ROSE

The seed is me
The stem rises free
A little water to grow
The legs start to glow

With a little sunlight I know
You and I will begin to show
As we open into a yellow rose
Never to hear the word no

Believing in your heart
As a petal comes apart
Giving you my best
Now let us both rest

Touch and then let go
Moist of a teardrop
Your voice soft and low
Saying don't, please stop

Wiping my petal as the drop falls down
Once again sweeping me off the ground
Into a yellow rose
Never to hear the word no

WHY NOT ME

Looking at each other
I pick up my feet
To make sure we do it together
We dance to the beat

You and I hold hands
Are we doing this right
I hope you understand
Does it matter tonight

Here comes another song
We got a chance
How can we go wrong
So let us dance
We are getting it on
But what about romance

One foot after another
Why not me
You and my sister
Why can't it be me

You like my sister
But let us dance again
I won't ask for another
Why not me instead of her

Here comes another song
We got a chance
How can we go wrong
So let us dance
We getting it on
But what about romance

Why not me
Why not me
Why not me

WHEN I WAS YOUNG

When I was young
I felt there was no fun
Sitting there staring at the wall
Didn't think anyone cared at all

I would watch the sun
And as the day was done
I would follow the light down
It always seemed to touch the ground

When I was young
I tried to waste my time
Sat alone losing my mind
I really never knew
That I could do as few
People did inside of me

Seeing the stars at night
Wonder how far, what a sight
Going out my window
Try to find the end of my rainbow

Oh when I was young
I was a tomboy with a gun
Playing with the guys' toys
Never knew it was only for boys

Taking my time thinking
Found myself dreaming
Of birds and the beauty of the pond
For I was the only girl up with the sun

When I was young
I never knew it could be done
I never knew that all it took
Was a simple little time with a book

When I was young
I felt I was the only one

WHO HAS A LIGHT

Who has a light
The flickering flame in my eyes tonight
I can see you striking up a match
Walking over with heat on your breath
Be careful not to blow me away
With the softness of your voice
In the cool air do I wanna stay
You reach me right here

Do you wanna match
Try to light up my fire
Don't leave with a smoking desire
I wanna feel each stick
Of your light not a burned stick
The burning match of the night
You by candlelight
Don't put me out
Let me slowly burn
Into your heart
Give me that head flickering start

Do you wanna match
Stop breaking that stick
Stick me up
Never touching the ground

Stop me from looking around
I wanna feel your beat
In the flame of the hot heat
Fingers on to the warm of your chest
While my head lays to rest
Do you wanna match
Try to light me up
Don't leave with a smoking desire
Feel the flame get higher
Never dying in wetness as a liar

You are the match, I'm the light
Smoking your last cigarette tonight
Never turning totally back
One last blow before I attack
Just burn into the night
Feeling the flame, the desire so right
Who has a light

August 24, 2009

WHATEVER

It used to be forever
Now it's whatever
LaLa LaLa Laid LA
LaLa LaLa Laid LA
Telling your story asking why
Finding out it's all a lie
LaLa LaLa Laid LA
I got to get on with my life
Say bye to my wife

Don't have any rush time to see the kids
Losing my mind over you, over you
LaLa LaLa Laid LA
LaLa LaLa Laid LA

I wish we could step back
Get back on the right track
Who says whatever

Whatever
No longer forever
Used to be my lover
It used to be forever
You and me lovers
Now it's whatever
LaLa LaLa Laid LA

Telling your story asking why
Finding out it's all a lie
LaLa LaLa Laid LA

I got to get on with my life
Say bye to my wife

Rushing to see the kids
Don't have any time
Over you, over you
Losing my mind
LaLa LaLa Laid LA

I wish we could go back
It's the end of the track

It used to be forever
You and me lovers
Now it's whatever
LaLa LaLa Laid LA

Whatever

Kick it to the curb, throw it out the window
Push it out the door, hit it against the floor
Hanging up

I AM NOT GOING TO CRY

I am not going to cry
No, no, not I
You set me free
Now I got to be me

But there is something wrong
What is going on
I really can't explain
But I can't complete

There is something missing
Something is very much missing
It's so hard to be free
I don't know how to be me

You have been there
Now you're not here
Somehow I am not scared
Yet I still care

But I am not going to cry
No, no, not I
I might see you in a crowd
But I won't cry out loud

I am not going to cry
No, no, not I

MY LEVEL

Now it is your turn
You're the one that's got to burn
You got to get up to my level
Now dude I am the devil

This time you'll be on your knees
This time you'll be the one saying please
Because Baby I am not going to start
So you can watch me fall apart

You gotta be good to me
You are the one that's going to let me be
I have now changed, I am not
Going to play those games

You stopped being an angel
So I am not going to be gentle
I am now going to be the devil
You got to get to my level
Baby this time it's your turn
Now you get on your knees and
Burn Baby BURN

You had me once
Now Baby I am out to lunch
You will have to try harder
You got to climb that ladder
You get to my level
I hate being the devil

TASTING RED LIPS

Not feeling the love on my lips
Being alone in the dark with your hips
Can you reach out with your voice
Giving yourself a choice
In your heart saying don't stop
The beat is in your two knees
Here's your chance, take off and meet
Feeling the pitter patter in my sound
My shoes dance around

You're getting closer and closer
Wanting the touch to be around
Take off into the street
Eyes connect in a parking lot
Felt the tongue against my teeth
Music in our ears
Tasting red lips
Now I'm really moving my hips

Going all the way on the floor
Wanting to feel somebody more
Roses in his hand loving that man
Soon he will be in my bedroom door

February 16, 2009

I AM CHECK'N

I am check'n
With you again
I could leave you if I tried
I just have too much pride

I am check'n
Once again
I really feel good inside
I follow your guide
My heart doesn't lie

I am check'n
Just loving you again
Give me my head spin
What did I win
Oh it's you again

I've been thinking of you
Can't get you off my mind
Off my heart, my soul
You are on a roll
My heart's just a boil
Don't want turmoil

I am check'n
Tell me when
Will I see you again

LIAR, LIAR
HIS PANTS ARE ON FIRE AGAIN

You say you're taking them
To your mother's, your sister's
And your brother's too
You never leave a right
Number yet, I know
Where to call you

You and I used to be on
Fire until I got burnt

The children don't want
To go, you say it's because
Of me
But we all know it's you

You never take them
Where you say you're going
They know it's another woman

Liar, liar
His pants are on fire again
Mom, do we have to go
He used to be my friend
Liar, liar, turn off
That frying pan

WHAT I LIKE

I like the morning sun
But you can't keep it still
It is usually on the run
It's just over the hill

I like the soft, warm skin
The words from an understanding man
If I find him I just might win
Just as long as he holds my hand

I like to finish what I start
To have an unexpected surprise
To handle a best part
Once in awhile would be nice

I like to put aside my gold
And just watch them grow
I really am not ready to be old
Just ready to flow

I like to have a friend to cry on
A mountain of love to set my mind
This way I know I am done
Staring into someone's eyes at times
I can see the stars come and go

It really is a pretty sight each night
But even when the lights are down low
There is nothing else but you that seems so right
You know my love will always be for you so

WE MADE IT ON THE 4TH

You run away
Days later you would say
I'm okay
But it hurt like hell anyway

Saying sorry, while I worried
Then came my birthday
You show up with a butterfly card
And hiding your tears
Sunglasses you let me later wear

Two days later
We counted candle numbers
I became a year older
Then two more days went by
All of you touch the sky
Going under the flag that was up so high
Feeling the tears go
You were your sunglasses, oh
Telling me I got to go
Picking me where you left off
I couldn't stop
While you run and hop
I tried to stop

We made it on the 4th
No matter how it poured
The sun was out as the clouds
Were in your eyes with doubts
We made it on the 4th
Together as a family
I could feel you say it's okay mommy
I just got to find my way
I am sorry you worried
But I can't play
I wanna be on my own today
I keep this picture of you touching the sky
With your brother and sister up high
Still wearing the sunglasses
Covering your tears in decades

March 6, 2009

DIMENSION

One by one they pass by
With a dented smile on their face
Try to beat the human race
Not to say a lie

Dimension turn into
Depression for two
Both you and I recreation
Loves interpretation

Hoping not to fade away
Giving one more day
To reach out and touch
Hoping never to be pushed

One by one they pass by
With a dented smile on their face
Try to beat the human race
Not to say a lie

Now we are back
Into dynamic love
You're always thought of

TWO THUMBS UP

I give you more than "two thumbs up"
Running through my mind all that happened
Last night and this morning was so
Wonderful, yet hard to believe every touch
Every moment with you was so dreamy
This morning felt so good inside
I just wanted more but as soon
As I hit the stairs
I knew the dream was over
And I had to get back home
I want it all to start again

Start again
Start again
Don't let the feeling end
You've become my closest friend

If I could make a dream
It would be like this
The hot steam
In your, in your kiss

Start again
Start again
Don't let the feeling end
I want yesterday here
I can't stop thinking of you
I want to be right there
With me saying yes will just do

WALKING ON LOGS

Through the woods over the rocks
Near the pond laid my socks
And you and I walking on logs
Don't push me off
Woo, woo, hold on, come on
Water in the air
Bend your knees without a care
Getting close to the edge
Almost there, you're dead
Jump to mine, God you're so fine

You and I walking on logs
You're such a tree guy, falling down, down
I step off and pick up my socks
And run, run off through the branches
You're all wet as I laugh

Can you catch me before I make it home
Arms out from behind
Around me touch the rush
Touch the rush of us
That's it

TRICK OR TREAT

Trick or treat
Let's you and I meet
You've got to be real sweet
Not some creep
Dancing to the ghost beat
Come closer and meet the mummy
All wrapped up in bandages and undrape me
Let yourself slide on in, doing it again
Don't scare me off my feet
Because I'm in heat, lets repeat
Full moon is out
Children all about
Are you in doubt
Scream and shout
Are you my vampire tonight
Take that bite of death out of me
Make my neck bleed as I come alive
Now you have arrived
With a piece of candy tonight
Now you have survived
In the dim light

For the boys
October 10, 2008

I WAS SWEET TILL SHE GOT AWAY

I was sweet till she got away
I really miss you
I wonder how you're doing

I'm trying hard to make my way
You gave me my step
And now you're gone
Somehow I will move on
I hope you found someone
Else who cares

Be strong because I used to love you
You gave me your all
I wish I kept five
With your number inside
Now I'm just staying alive

Wishing you were mine
In my heart
But I just keep falling apart
Now I am on the side of the street
I want a new start

I was sweet till she got away

TOUCHING THE NUMBNESS

Touching the numbness
Having a dry throat
Not being able to choke
Seeing your breath
Wiping a tear
Knowing you care

I have been there
Endless nights with you
I took that ticket
When you say I do
Please don't tell me we are through

Touching the numbness
Hearing the kindness
In my heart you
Are a part of me
But now you and I
Are set free

In the air
I am still there
But you are not here
Beside me
I was set free

TOUCH MY G STRING

Touch my G string
And I'll do my thing
With your fingers running down my neck
I get naked to the touch of each fret
Hearing each sound
When through your love I have found

A vertical smile that's made me wild
I feel tenderness running for miles
In your pick it gets harder each time

Touch my G string
And I'll do my thing
Naked to the sound
Each beat we are fooling around
Got to get down

THERE'S NO WAY I CAN DO

There's no way I can do
The love dove part

I don't want to be done
Well tell me that I can
Move on
Then come back
I want you for so long

You know I don't
I'll see you this weekend
Wear your leather jacket
I don't need it
Here's your coat

Why do you still put your
Hat on backwards
So you notice me
My clothes are still
Bagged but they fit
Me just the same

There's no way I can do
The love dove part
I didn't think anyone
Loved me, it was
My fault now I
Know my
Mom and dad, brother, sister,
Grandma and grandpa
Have a heart I can say I will
I do

SUGAR AND SPICE FIRE AND ICE

Kiss me and taste the sugar
Touch me and feel the spice
The heat hits the fire
No longer cold as ice

Releasing all the pain
Restore the lover flames
As you melt in my arms now
I will show you how

No more turmoil
Our hearts beginning to boil
Sugar and spice
Fire and ice
Temperature on high
Reaching paradise in the dim light

TELL SOMEONE ELSE

Here I am in a fight
Still there's nothing that seems right
I wonder if they remember the tears
I wonder if they ever come here

I wanted it to stop
They just keep on bringing it to the top
Fight, fight
It just ain't right
Will I make it through the night

Now they are gone
But deep inside the tears still go on
I try to forget
Then I can't help remembering the fit

Why do I got to keep on going with you
Try to explain but will he give in
How are we ever going to win
Do you think we will be friends again

Sisters, brothers hold each other
Cool it's over love one another
Tell me I am here to listen
Don't wait until she comes home
God did not help
Just like a drink won't

So don't give up on yourself
Tell someone else

TAKE THAT STEP

I want to meet
That girl who can
Take that step
And give me one, just like that
Show me her love
Under the spotlight
With just one touch
I want it so much

The way she moves
Gives me the grooves
And fills me with chills
Seeing her eyes, without any lies

Take that step
And you will have more steps
Your love will live on
Moving on so strong
Making music in your step
Making love in our hearts
Falling and sliding apart
Into someone's lap

Take that step
And give me one, just like that

November 27, 2008

DANCING WITH YOU ONLINE

Dancing with you online
Make my phone move to the sound
Of music and when I hear you
In my ear I feel the beat
That I want to meet
And be a part of that heart
So try to steal mine
Get me back online
In Spokane

March 22, 2009

REMEMBER FIRST LOVE

I remember the look in your eyes
The way you said goodbye
I hold your letters close to me
I am hoping to come and see you
Just like it should always be
You and I in love, Ya

Love at first sight I saw
The tears stop when you call
You holding me close
I try to hold on like a post
Picture of folded hands see love
See two people, you and I, you thought of

I sit there thinking about you
And just can't forget what we used to do
Now we are both gone
We have not seen each other in so long

I touch your picture wishing you were here
Even those down deep in my heart you're there
But still there I feel love to say I care
David remember always in my heart
You out of them all I will never part

David remember first love you always
You I love I will always say
Baby I just can't wait 'til tomorrow
For all the sorrows

I love you more than ever
More than just a lover
Just hold me and never let go
Please David let it be so

David remember first love always
You I love is what I always say
The folding hands
You and I as one

The way we both understand
David some day it will be done
Yes you and I as one
David remember first love always
You and I call it love babe

SHE'S JUST TOO OLD

I wanted her so
Come back to me
She said we are through
Let me be free

I miss my sheet dress
And pillowcase hat
And her fuzzy teddy bear
Alarm that went off with a care

I miss her nightie
And the strings
And her love hair
And tummy

I love rubbing my feet
Against her toes
Touch her thighs
And rubbing her nose

I miss her lips
As we kiss so lightly
Down her neck
I want her back

She was just too old
I was told

TAG ME ALIVE

Listening to your greeting
As you listen to mine
Just words passing in between lines
Leaving each other the same thoughts
Open to tag me alive
Before your minutes go by
You say we are playing phone tag
You don't say you're it
Instead you say your number
I say, I've got it, pushing each one in
Now saying you've tagged me alive
You whisper these soft words
But I say I just don't know
Speeding up the words
Hoping not to lose the missing piece
Voice became quiet
Tag me alive
The phone line is now silent
Yet both of us are still on the line
Hearts pump in the dark
Tag me live
Music began to play as I heard you say
Let's do it Sunday, you hit me alive, Sunday arrive
Now your tag has touched my skin and then
Touch you alive with my phone hand and
No phone but still the words I hear in my ear
I heard on line, you're tagging me alive

February 8, 2009

NOTICING ME

I was born in 1965
I never knew I could survive
But as I grew
I found out what I could do

I watched the beauty of the
Sunlight in the morning air
Growing up I found love and
The gentleness of him
So many times getting hurt from them

As the days went on
I did something wrong
But I felt it in my heart
And learn how to do a new start

I got older I got scared
Wondering if I could find
Someone who would care
Would he always be there

The darkness of the night
I would sit and watch the
Stars come in slowly each
So beautiful and bright

The older I got
Seems like I want a lot
I brought back memories
And remember each of life's stories

Then before I knew it
I was asleep dreaming it
Then as I woke
I couldn't find the words unspoken

I thought 1965
Now I am so glad to be alive
Noticing me
I am glad to be me

MY TEARDROP

Well today is Sunday
One year ago on this very day
After two months and two days we broke up
As I put coffee in my cup

I give you a call
You answer and telling me it all
I loved you then
I love you still now
And I just don't know how

Life is so hard
But I feel you are not far
Tears come down my eyes
Why I try to let you realize

That I love you now
And I loved you then
I just don't know how

To tell you goodbye

You tell me to stop crying
But I just keep on trying

To tell you how much I miss
How much I wish for one more kiss
All the memories lay inside of us today
I wish we were together in some way

Because I love you now
I loved you then
And I just don't know how
To let us be on again

Time has changed somehow
So I want to say
I love you now
I love you still after today

Just let my tears drop
Just let them stop

HITTING THE 18TH MARK

Time to go on your own
Remember when you were walking
At nine months holding on
Getting into everything
Now you're up and gone
Cruise in the car everywhere
Hoping not to hit anything
Like you did when you were nine
Showing off for your sweetie

Getting a job is so hard
Saving money, is it in your cards
Trying to slow down
When friends are near
Soon you will be all alone
Hope not too far
Doing your crazy hair mood
Losing your moon ring dude

Hitting the 18th mark
Here's the key to your heart
You're going to miss me
Can't you see I want you to be free

You're going to call home soon
I'll be waiting for the phone call
Around noon
Remember your first dance
Now you've got that chance

Hitting the 18th mark
Here are the keys to your car
We love you, you will go far
Make it good whoever you are

To Kyle at 18th
April 27, 2008

PAIN FROM OUR KNUCKLES

Pain from our knuckles
We have a lot of
Trying no more of
This painless love

Fighting to get it right
When there is no wrong
Yet wanting to belong
To carry on

Taste our blood
Feel the abuse
No longer used
Walking away
Reaching for another day

Tears hit my spin
When you are out of line
Sadness stays
We used to love and play
Now we both pay
I still want you after today
I let you go anyway

December 3, 2008

MOMMY EVEN THO

Mommy even tho
I may be two
This song is for you

As I grow through
See what I can do
Dancing so little fast
In my toddler jeans at last

Mommy even tho
I may be two
My hair up in curls
I am still your little girl

Doing a twirl
With a mike in my hand
Pretend to sing as I swing
Feeling the beat, still being sweet

Trying to snap my fingers
Using my voice as a singer
Mommy this song is for you
Even tho I may be two

I'm growing through you
My eyes may be blue
Shining as you look
I'm your brook

Mommy this song is for you
I can do it now at two

MORNING STILL

7 a.m. open my eyes
Now I know who I am
Last night was dim
In one night I realize

Morning still
You are so real
There is more than those lips
Summer in winter blitz

Kindness hits my fingertips
Oh mmm, oh mmm, yes
Don't let me go, not a second no
Oh mmm, oh mmm, I said no

Now it's tomorrow
Pull me back into the covers
You're not leaving yet
No one sorrow
Voices over the phone
The morning still
You're so real
There is more than those lips
Summer in winter blitz

DO YOU LOVE ME

Do you love me
Is this the way it's going to be
I give you gifts and love
I make a wish on the stars above
You give me a kiss goodbye
As I sit here and wonder why

Walk away and take
Leaving me still here awake
The tears came down
How many tears do I wait
To put my feet on the ground
Will I be too damn late

I don't want people to see my face
Somehow my heart is out of place
You take and make all the space
But tell me how to win with you Ace

I found myself on my own
Me always ending up alone
I need your love right here
How come you seem not to care

Do you love me
It's so hard to see
I found myself alone
Once again on my own
Got to wait
Once again too damn late

Do you love me
Are you going to let it be

LOOK ME IN THE EYE

Look me in the eye
Are you afraid you might
Like me again
That was, was not me
This is me now can't you see
I want to be me later and free

Look me in the eye
Drink up with the guy
Filled my toes with getting high
You see me almost die

Red dress around my neck
Are you still in luck
Lets ride, ride on the Harley
Feel the breeze in my hairly

Look me in the eye, when
Are you loving me again
Can we try to survive
Feel our love so alive

LAYING IN HER BED

Laying in her bed
Felt the love that wasn't there
Watch her TV
Laid my head on her pillow
Saw the pictures on her dresser
Somehow I felt less than her

Smelling her perfume
Saw right through the mirror
Another her, me
Alone in my room

Yet I didn't want to leave her bed
I saw all the joy we both have
Our children faces
I felt I was in the right place
In her space

Now we've become such great friends
As we still look for our man
Keeping our children hands clean
Let's go out dirty girlfriend
You can wear my earrings
We now share the same things

December 8, 2008

UNDER THE CHRISTMAS LIGHTS

He said I wanta do it
Under the Christmas lights
I want to be your package tonight
Wearing a ribbon and a purple bow
See the lights in your hair
As I unwrap my gift
I want it tonight
Please don't make me wait

I look up and see our glowing star
Colorful stocking on the wall
My gift may be small, go ahead unwrap me
But you're on my list
Touching you my heart skips a beat
Looking at the trimming I felt the heat

There was no fireplace
But we didn't need it anyway
I could see our faces in bulbs
Pictures of our children on the table
But was I in the right place
Looking into your eyes we kissed
Feeling your skin with the ribbon
In her hair and the bow on my chest
We begin to laugh and smile
The sparkle came back so fast
What I wish for is you
My love is still true

December 7, 2008

LOST MY LOOSE JEANS

Lost my loose jeans
They were a nice fit
I was in a daydream and
She gobbled me away

She really cared for me
Now what do I do
I wanted so much to say I do
But she had a family that's not mine
I guess I was too scared
To get involved with her children
And fall in love with her
I miss her so tight around me
Loose and free in loose jeans
She was so busy but she had time for me
Wanted all her time, but I would not give her mine
Her children had somewhat of a father
And I didn't know how to become a dad
Now I want to try but I don't know where she's at

Lost my loose jeans
They were a nice fit
I was in a daydream and
She gobbled me away
She really cooked
And pulled my hook and jerk
I was the jerk who got hooked
She asked me for my first kiss
And touched me like this

LOOKING FOR LOVE
THAT FLOATS UP

I've been alone for 9 years
Made it through all the fears
Looking for love that floats up
I still fill my own cup

In all my pain
Is there ever a gain
Can a man bring me flowers
Lay back holding me for hours

Take care of the little things
Leave me in the shower to sing
Notice my kids
Let him do what I did

Looking for love that floats up
I want you to fill my cup
With two jobs and bills
I'm running down several hills

Reaching out for your hand
Where is that man
Let's do it till dawn then talk
Together you and I will walk

Hand in hand we share
I want love to be fair
Looking for love that floats up
Let's fill more than us in a cup

August 18, 2008

ECLIPSE

I look around
Feeling totally down
All alone in the car
Just driving nowhere far

Darkness coming over me
Stopping the car I couldn't see
Silence, no place to go
I don't understand the unknown

Reach for the radio
Find myself alone
Wanting to get back home
The eclipse is now here
Who in the hell out there cares

A dark and dusty place
So much room for a space
Moon, stars, not even a sun
Again finding myself on the run
Who could tell if it was day or night
Who turned out the lights

Reach for the arctic
Find myself alone
Wanting to get back home
The eclipse is now here
Who in the hell out there cares

IN A SPIDERMAN WHEELCHAIR

I walked in seeing this family
With a little boy smiling and his eyes
Staring right at me
All around his wheelchair
Was a Spiderman blanket of care
So I wrote this for him

No matter where or who you are
You are somebody in someone's eyes
This is for you down deep inside
A wheelchair Spiderman that can fly
I know your web is right there in disguise

So reach up high
Go ahead and wheel yourself to the sky
By a web that takes your smile away
Making it in a flying chair
With a family bringing you there

Your family may be on a string
But I am feeling everything
Touching your blanket that sets you free
A small hero wheeling in our eyes
By a web that takes your smile away
Making it in a flying chair
With a family bringing you there

Down deep this is your time to fly
Go ahead and wheel yourself to the sky
By a web that takes your smile away
Bring it to your family as their hero
In a Spiderman wheelchair reaching high
I can see you giving all you can under Spiderman
Seeing the web around you, holding your mom's hand
See your dad smile, holding on tight again

March 12, 2009

MAKING PEACE WITH YOU

Here I am
Making peace with you
What to say or do
I am so in love with you
Come on don't be blue
I've only loved a few

Wow your broken heart
Need a new start
I'm back
Rushing to you at last
Don't give up that fast

Making peace with you
Come on don't be blue
What to say or do
I've only loved a few

Put your hand in mine
Now I have all the time
In your world
You're my girl, my girl

SADDLE IT UP WITH A BOUNCE

Saddle it up with a bounce
Give us that hoop of responsibility
See us move every ounce
Into the net of successes

In our own different way
Their time for horseplay
Let's ride, bouncing that ball
Growing up nice and tall

Saddle it up, saddle it up
With a bounce
Two different brothers
And a cowgirl sister

Reaching up high
Riding on by
Giving each a part of the sky
You are the reason why

Saddle it up with a bounce
Don't sit on the couch
Make something of yourself
Try it, just be yourself

February 17, 2009

LAST DAYS WITH MY DAD

You adopted us giving love
A mom and dad and star above
We grew with a future of our own
Never left to do it alone

Then it happened last year
When you fell
We all rushed to be there
As you went through hell

I felt I was at a loss
As you lay there and tossed
You, holding on, saying goodbye
Days later, you're still alive

Back and forth you came
There was so much pain
Finding out who you are
As my tears begin to fall
Last days with my dad
I never really understood you
Feeling so deep and sad
Now I really do ...

THANK YOU, THANK YOU

March 14, 2002

JUST TELL ME WHEN

He was the only boy
Still giving his mom joy
His children deep inside
Not leaving them behind

Tell me about his life
Shaking his head about his ex-wife
Looking at me with those eyes
I'm trying, trying
Touching and dying

Words are coming out wrong
Yet I'm trying to hold on
He was the only boy
His dad's pride and joy

I'm acting like a fool
But he says he has
The right tool
Feeling a little uncool
I tell him it was just a line
He says I don't mind

I start to touch him
He says just tell me when
Walking away I can hear him say
Just tell me when

Just tell me when
Now he is here again

IF YOU COULD ONLY UNDERSTAND

If you could only understand
If you could only read my mind
Just take my hand
And see the way I do my time

Just take my hand
Watch me grow and live
Please only understand
I've got to make my own drive

Down, down the lonely road
Find my own life
Without you cutting like a knife
Down, down this lonely road

If you could believe in me
Just let my world be
I've got to learn to survive
Make it through this world alive

But I will make my mistakes
And yes that's what it really takes
So please for Heaven's sakes
Take my hand and understand
I have what it makes

If you could believe in me
Just let my world be
I've got to learn to survive
Make it through this world alive

I'VE LOST YOU

I feel pain in here
Hurting me everywhere
I've lost you for good
This is hard for me to do

Saying goodbye, goodbye to you
I've loved you so much
Losing you, your love, your touch
Goodbye I must, goodbye to you

We have come to an end
Forward, forward, I'm letting you go
No turning back, goodbye
Getting off the railroad tracks

All we have now is our children
We need to give them all we can
You have someone else to love
I'm letting your wings fly like a dove
Goodbye I must, goodbye to you
Fly away, fly away
Goodbye to you after today
You are gone
Goodbye Randy

I'M SORRY I HUNG UP

I'm sorry I hung up
I kind of fell asleep

There is an evening
When I say just talk
And you think that a
Negative thing

I really do love you
I know I do

You know I love
Your tone

It's pretty to me
Didn't I tell you that
Now say something dreamy

I love your tone
Just let me dream
Until Sunday afternoon
When my eyes wake up, beam
I'm sorry I hung up
I kind of fell asleep
I don't want to sweep
Over you, over you
Just want to love your tone

IF YOU LET HIM
HE WILL HURT YOU

He's married, he doesn't
Care about anything
But himself
If you let him
He will hurt you
Let me back in

But I'm tired of old news
Don't do it you're
Giving me the blues

You're still married
But his touch I need tonight
Don't you know I still
Love you so
Is this wrong of Mr. Right

I need a new kick
In my life
But don't you have security
What's wrong with you and me

Now I don't need to
Fall in love again
Know what I'm missing
Is you not him

I'M NOT A BLOND BUT YOU I CAN TOUCH

But I'm touching you
Because you said I would do
Playing in the bathroom
Gotta go touch
Before I flush

I really didn't need to go
I just followed her in
To touch, touch her again
A little dirty thing walking in
But why worry, not me baby
You wipe my tears
Holding me in front of the mirror
Give me that hold on my tush
So honey before I flush
Let's you and I go touch

Later washing as you looked hard
Inside of me with those eyes
You let me touch more than
The next girl
I got the hat
In tennis shoes, flats
She has that skirt
That's short and black
A blue zip-up shirt
That touches me in the sack

We give the guys our look
And take each other shook
Then we take one more move
As they look at her boots
Follow us wanting to touch
But we just look at them
And just, just flush
I want, I want touch
Before I flush
You give me a mirror head rush
So push, push the wipe tonight
And wash away my tears
With that tush, squeezing there
I can make it with you double wipe care
Let's put the handle on him as we flush
I wanta, I wanta touch

I'M TRYING TO GET TO HEAVEN

I'm trying to get to heaven
So I can date the lord
After the first date
He said I'm his, oh god
And then the devil walked on in

With fire in his hands
Then I reached for the stars
Getting higher and higher
Soon I was up in the clouds
With a hot liar

It began to rain and I
Cooled his ass down
I ended up on the ground
Don't fret we stayed up all night

But by the crack of dawn he was gone
I'm trying to get to heaven
Dancing around in my loose gown
Looking for that lord of peace
Soon he will see it in my eyes

Saying I'm his, oh god again
Then we will be in heaven
And back on the ground doing it again and again

I'M USED TO TWO

I'm used to two
You crazy fool
Only use that tool on me
So let's connect
And get the effect
Before you reject
Come on let's pour it on
Before I'm gone

It's kinda of cold
And refreshing
So say it again
In the wind
Play with it on it
I'm wishing again

Huh huh huh

How to feel
Like still, like still
Restless in the kill

I'm used to two
You crazy fool
Let's show what we can do
I'm holding, holding, on to you

I JUST MET YOU

I just met you
Already I feel brand new
You are really so nice
I feel like I am in paradise

I really want to get to know you
I feel that you will make it too
Let's dance
Dance to the music
Let's dance
Dance to the music now

Step to step we'll groove to the motion
Step to step we'll move like the ocean
Let's dance
Dance to the music
Let's dance
Dance to the music now

I think we've got it
Dance, dance, you've shown us how
I think we've got it now
More to learn to the groove
More to learn, let us move

I am glad we have this time
I wonder what's on your mind
Word for word we'll get it together
Word for word soon we'll know one another
So far we've made it in the play
I hope we can make it through the next day
Dance, dance to the music
Dance, dance to the music

More to learn, we've got it together
Word for word now we know one another
Step to step we will know it forever

I'M YOUR LOVE, LOVE PAD

I'm your love, love pad
Treat me oh so bad
It's not what you say
That makes me stay
It's how low you can go
I want to say no
The way you go down
God I wanta fool around

Then you lift me up
Twist me like a top
I feel your heart and soul
My nipples are getting hard and cold

I'm your love, love pad
Don't leave me oh so sad
Touch me here and there
Give it to me everywhere

I'm your love, love pad
Treat me oh so bad
I'm your love, love pad
Don't leave oh so sad

All I want to do is play
Let me have my way
Close your eyes dear
I will always be near

To Alex Arich
October 10, 2008

I HAVE NO CLUE, DO YOU

I have no clue but I hope it's you
See a world through a glass window
Wanting deep inside to hear hello
You begin to run then you rock and roll
I have no clue do you

I try so hard to prove I am me
I need to slow down so I can see
I have no clue in who I want to be
But I know I am just me

I love you so dearly, mom
For all you have done
But we both need to rest
Slow down, do one thing at a time

I have no clue but I am so glad you are you
Let's take one step at a time
Give each other a peace of mind
Laughter and holding are joy
Listening to each other's tears
I have no clue, do you
Thank you for loving me too

FREE FROM ME

Do you really need me
I hope to be
With you forever
Keep me warm my lover

I feel for love
But what are you thinking of
Do you really want to hold me
Are you the person I really see

You're so gentle and tender
I don't want to forget
Just hold you and remember
Be with you that's it

I feel for you each day
I want to believe in what you say
I really want to be there
To just say I care

You're always on my mind
Each and every time
I am not sure why
I don't want to say goodbye
Do you really want me
Do you really want to care
Would you like to be
Just free from me
I just want to be
With you
Do you want me too

FALL FOR YOU

Fall for you
Yesterday I was falling for you
Just say Hello
And I don't want to say no
Fall for you I have
And yes I am glad

If only you could fall too
How can I be with you
Stare at you all day
Daydreaming of what you will say
So why don't you

Just want to go out
That's all I think about
I fall for you
If you would fall too
The things we could do

Now I am just wishing
I am just hoping about you
That you would fall too

I can't live without
Since that date
That's all I talk about

I fall for you
Why don't you fall too

HELP MY FRIEND DON'T TAKE HER

She's sitting there holding a string
Don't let go, don't let her go, please
Rescue her, give her a second chance
Let all this pain pass as romance

Help my friend/lover/husband
She says to me I want to dance
Don't know father, mother
She's all I got don't take her

The children are so young to understand
Give her time to be with them again
Let each one know she loves them so
Rescue her from all this pain
Stop! Stop! Don't take her in the rain

Bring out the sun, bring her home
I don't want my own again
Help me, friend, husband
Don't take her, give her this dance
She is all I've got, just let her win
This one more time take a breath again
Can she wake up and say I'm here to stay friend

STRAWBERRY HILL

Fishes in the pond
You and I giving a little
Just a moment hold one
Will we ever settle

Getting wet in the sun
Showing me Strawberry Hill
Touch as you feel the thrill
Still on the run

Dry off with a damp cloth
Your heart in the right spot
The story we could tell
Just think of Strawberry Hill

Strawberry Hill
Strawberry Hill
If you need me
I am there

HIGH OFF LIFE

Feelings that I never had before
Are happening more and more
Getting high off life
Now isn't that nice
You kind of want to pay the price
Oh, oh yes, isn't that nice

Now you and the stars are up there
Are making me see down here
Life, you and I
High off life
Now that's really nice

Yes we are two high off life
You and I
Now we know it isn't love
Just what we see above

Things I never felt before
I don't want to close the door
Just getting high off life
Is a lot better than
Cutting yourself with a knife

As you can see then
It's just you and I
And we won't die
Just getting high off life
Now that's really nice

Yes, you and I high off life
You and I

HERE'S TO A GIRL THAT DIDN'T GET IT

Here's to a girl that didn't get it
I'm right here after all
I know you are always on time
Even though your alarm clocks jumps
You still keep on hopping

Doing all you can to win him
Giving your all as he runs
Showing your love then you fall again
Hoping for true friendship

Dealing with his lies
As you lie next to him
Seeing in his eyes, you surprise you

HER OR ME

I made up my mind
Now you gotta pick up that line
You see it's her or me
You can't have every girl you see
I cannot let that be
It's her or me

You told me about her ways
Still you're not sure about today
Maybe she can handle it
But I have been through it before
And believe me she will have a fit
I am not taking it anymore

Tell her it's over between us
We are just friends
Forget the big fakes
There is no way I will win
Because I know
I am not good enough for you
So I've got to let you go
I know that this is true

Instead of going crazy
I'll part like a daisy
Please just go
Before I say please, no
You've got a mind to make up this time
I have said the last words of my line

It's her or me
Even then you're not sure of what you see
This is the way it's got to be
So take her instead of me
I know how it would be
Just let us be friends
Because I know I am not going to win

THE DAYS GO BY

Waking up with your hand on my skin
Turning over to hold you once again
Memories of trying to be together
Hardly finding time to see one another

Picking you up for afternoon lunch
Noticed in a short time we could touch
Memories when you came over half asleep
Somehow you always came through, our love so deep

Feeling the breeze coming through the window
Remember in my ear you gave a soft blow
You know I will always love you so
As you once again get up and go

The days go by
Thinking of you and I cry
Without you I would die
Just memories of you go by

HE IS GONE

Something exciting
Is here not gone
The growing pain
Is a shot of a gun

Now the excitement
Is now growing pain
For all that is sent
I have gone insane

He is gone
But not too far
For we are still one
Yes we still are

I must go on
With my lonely life
No matter if it was wrong
If it was bad or nice

I must go on
For there was tonight
I know it was not long
And it didn't turn out right

Stay as one
Love in spirit is here
For you are now gone
I know you are near

I know you are in heaven
With the Lord above
I will never forget your lov'n
And you I will always think of

HE KNEW A FRIEND

He knew a friend that gave her
Email address

On Father's Day I ask what my
Husband wants, he said a computer
I gave him Web TV
Now he just sits there

Tells her all these stories
About his children
And me
How much he loves me
And to let him be

She would say you believe
Her
Yes I know she loves me so
She's taking the kids away to
See her real brothers
Oh brother
You still believe her I
Can babysit them
She took them
Anyway

Now I live at my mom's home
With my children still trying to find
That man and I've seen my brothers
Again
He's still with her yet
He has a fiancée too

GETTING HER FEET DIRTY

Both hard workers
With aching muscles
Knees always bending
Pain in back hurting
Getting her feet dirty
Ending in a hurry

You having the same desire
Feeling good being higher
After wanting that soak
Bubbles bare on a float
Rubbing those toes
Seeing me without pantyhose

Stretching down on my back
Nails against our skins
Forgetting the past
Holding at last when

Music easing both minds
Relaxing in time
Is there a dirty blond on line
Who has a bottle of wine
Auburn, 44, deep blue, 5 foot 7,
Curves and more
Feet on the bare floor

Dripping oil down smooth as it sound
Wishing you were always around
Getting her feet dirty
Running home in a hurry
Is there a dirty blond on line
I want him to be mine

September 5, 2009

GETTING LOST WHILE FINDING HIM

Getting lost while finding him
As he wanders around, try to find you
In another view of love
The image of his past hoping for
    THE FUTURE

But we both seem to get lost
In the space that isn't there
Not see a breath of air
That we take each
    SECOND

As we touch another one's love
Feeling the soft skin
Is there a never landing end
    KISS

Getting lost, finding him
Is a running battle
Stopping the wind
With your hand
Holding onto his
    ARMS

Actually feeling
What is not here
Until you reach her
    IN THE AIR

YOUR LIFE

I look into your eyes
Have you ever realized
How your weekend begins
And how it ends

Do you feel the same each day
Or do you change in many ways
Is your mind on many things
Do you see your life as a dream
Is life the way it really seems

If you could take a day
And do it your way
Like a play
Would you at all change
How would you rearrange
Your life, make you feel so right
All the way through the night

If you could stop time
Would you think it's a crime
Just to be in a different place
Just to have some time and space
Would your mind at all settle
With a little make believe could
You at all tell

Your life is so hard to live
How am I going to find a place to give
Your life makes you feel so right
Does my kiss have to end with goodnight

Your life, how is it
Could I try to fit

YOU SAY YOU HAVE A FIANCÉE

You say you have a fiancée
But when you pick up your children
You take them to another woman
You say you take care of them on your own
Not alone

It used to be me
Now she is in my shoes
And I am set free
Still blue

The women have children too
I'll never understand you
While you go from one to the other
Say you're a dad not a father

I still think you're a boy
And we are your toy
At least I am
With the feet on the ground
You won't bring me down

You say you have a fiancée
Someday you will get
Child support and you will pay
Then you won't be so hot

Real soon someday
Child support you will pay
And I will have my day

FORGET ME NOTS

Forget me not his name, his face
Forget me not his kiss, his warm embrace
Forget me not the love that you once knew
Remember now, he loves someone new

Forget me not the love that you once shared
Forget me not the fact that he once cared
Forget me not the time when you were together
Remember now, he's gone forever

Forget me not him when they play your song
Forget me not how you cried the whole night long
Forget me not how close you once were
Remember now, he's loving her

Forget me not how often he used to phone
Forget me not the times you were alone
Forget me not he's just your whole wide world
Remember now he loves that girl

Forget me not the way he held your hand
Forget me not the way he'd understand
Forget me not the guy that has your heart
Remember now you're far apart

Forget me not the memory you both shared
Forget me not the way he brushed your hair
Forget me not the way he used to hold you at night
Forget me not he kissed your ear, neck, and hips
Forget me not him, now you've said goodbye
Remember now, you mustn't cry

FINGERPRINTS ON YOUR PANTS

Fingerprints on your pants
I'm feeling as I dust them off
Should I slap and take on the task
There goes my top
I don't want to stop

Hands going down your striped shirt
Wanting it to hurt
In your jeans
You look rough and mean

But I'm still feeling the beat at 1 a.m.
Your butt is in
As we kiss and pretend
Nicely dressed up
Ripping off you jump
Fingerprints on your pants

Should I slap
Taking the task
I'm feeling as I dust them off

FAKE IT
MAKE IT

Started going to many meetings
Heard it would work
Stop it, didn't believe
Try it, didn't drink any
Fake it

Rush on back
Beginning to listen in
Got up to explain
Actually hear their stories
Miss a day, skip one
Didn't think about a drink
Fake it

Now I can honestly
Say it's been 288 days
And I'll make it
Through this year
Without you I would
Fake it

I WILL NEVER BLINK

I will never blink
Even tho you sink
Down, down into me
I'm still running free

Don't go the other way
I want you to stay
I don't want to be confused
Go ahead and use

I will never blink
Even tho you sink
Into my love free
You still holding onto me

Feel every breath rough
Don't feel my touch me so tough
I will never blink
Even tho you sink
Into my love free
Hold on to me

And go ahead sink
Down, down into me

EVERY WHICH WAY

I do not lie
I never say goodbye
To my guy
Not at all, no not I

Every which way
Each and every day
They go every which way
Just flowing away

I do not walk by
It's an open sky
I listen and believe
Hoping they think of me

Another one comes along
And then soon he is gone
I am not sure why
But I never say goodbye

Every which way
Each and every day
It happens again
Somehow I am still their friend

Letting him walk out the door
Saying I don't want it like this anymore
And holding on deep inside
You know he really lied

Every which way
We must go on today
No matter what they say
He will soon flow away

DEBBIE

It was in March when I
Thought of you
I looked about and saw
People I knew
But I wonder about you
Would you make it through

I closed my eyes
And saw you there inside
I hoped you would be all right
Thinking of you in my dreams at night

Now you are there
Remember I really care
Girl get well soon
I will be here this afternoon

I bring for you blue carnations
Just keeping an old generation
Hold on to your dreams
Keep life the way it seems

We will be together
As one my friend
Until the end

So hold on tight
As I go away
Thinking of you through the night
And I will remember this day

CRUNCHING DOWN

Crunching down
Still looking at her
I'm not sure
How to tell her

I may be mature
But I had to snip
Snip, snip, snip
Before I snap

No more kids for me
I want to be free
She said let me be
I guess I screwed up again
It was worth it in the end

Screwing up is kind of fun
Trying hard to do is under the sun
I've had slappy sex
And end up blue
With another child or two
I love both no matter what I do

Crunching down
Looking at you
I'm still screwing up
Saying I've been snip, snip woo
Go ahead and screw me dooo

CRYSTAL BALL INSIDE ME

Crystal ball inside me
what do I see
A man taller than me
Out the door set me free
Not a word to me

Close my eyes I still see
A mist of smoke taller than me
He gave me life to live
He gave me heart to give
He gave me peace of mind
He gave me all his time

Now he gives me freedom and a sigh
But somehow I'm lost in these dandelions
Three more times
Then you came along and walked me through
Yet I still see him in the dew
Now I know it's time to say I Do
As you take my hand and say I Love You too

Morning, day, night to dawn
A smoke, a mist, a light brings me you
Life live, heart give, peace of mind
Time, sign, you walk me through
Now there's just dew but I'm safe with you

WARM FROM YOUR FORM

There are times when I am warm
Just from your form
When you get close to me
My hands don't want to be free

Holding on to you
Hold me baby please do
I am warm for your form
My heart is being torn
Just never let me go
Oh baby please no

Take me up on this chance
Our night just for romance
You and I
Close your eyes
It will all come true
I just want to be with you

Warm from your form
My heart is being torn
For you to hold on
Hoping this won't go wrong

BE NOT AFRAID

Be not afraid, in time
You will be mine
You and I understand
We need to be loved again

Just like a balloon
High up we go and blooming
Wind blowing in our faces
Seeing so many places

We will fly high
Up, up into the sky
Be not afraid in time
I still want you in mind

Looking down at the world
What we have been through
I still want you, want you

Giving from the tip
Taking time to stop
Feel the heat, the wind
Feel you once again

Be not afraid
I still love you today
Now go on your way
Friendship every weekday
Including Saturday and Sunday

BE WITH YOU

The sunshine in my eyes
You on my mind
Why can't you and I
Ever find some time
To see each other
Spend time together

You and I
I never realize
How much I care
God
I wish you were here

The closer we get together
The more I'd rather
I really want to
Be with you

Time you look out on me
I was there to be
Only to be with you
And to look up at the view
Just to be with you
I really want to be

So hold me in your arms
And I will never forget your charm
Just close friends
You and I it won't end
You and I never realize

Be with you
I really want to
Be with you

ACQUAINTANCE

We were just acquaintances
A form of love and romances
You found yourself
So close but remember someone else

You soon left me behind
Without losing any time
I found you in her arms
I was not at all alarmed

You were just acquaintance
Taking your chances
And found yourself
Remembering someone else

I know you really love her
I was told by another
Now that I've looked at you
I know your love is true

I will remember this acquaintance
I will remember the chances
Now go to her and love will come
As I will remember we had some

But only acquaintance
Left to many chances
Love was here you know
And even though you must go
I really don't feel so low

Just acquaintance
Taking your chances
For me to you
To her I do

Just acquaintance
Little romances
Left to many chances

PARACHUTE

The plane is about to crash
You hand me a parachute
We jump out at last
Will this love suit

Should I count to ten
Pull the string and then
Let my feet back on the ground
Or will you end up letting me down

All of a sudden I am in the air
I have all this fear right here
This suit of love
I am not sure of

I look straight down
Closing my eyes I hit ten
Will you be around
Or is this the end

The plane is about to crash
You gave me a parachute
We jump out at last
Will this love suit
Pull the string
Is this my thing

I finally touch the ground
You were there still around
Parachute put my feet down
And you were found

TAKING CARE OF HIS OWN WORLD

Taking care of his own world
While he's in mine plus our children combined
To show they're one-of-a-kind
Before I take his hand and
Walk down that line

I want to say I Do one last time
Giving our children a peace of mind
Filling their hearts with love
I want our hands to fit like a glove
Hoping for the same
I will take your last name

Death do us part
Is a lot for my heart
But trying it again
I hope he is more than a friend
A man tying the knot to the end
Taking care of his own world
While he's in mine plus our children combined
To show they're one-of-a-kind
Before I take his hand
And walk down that line
Now my last name is the same
Married for the third time

February 16, 2009

CALL HOUSE BLUES

In the middle of December
As we went through November
You said you never had enough
Come on and give me some love

On the phone is a soft voice
I felt I had no other choice
I guess you don't know how to start
By not coming you broke my heart

You said to give you time
In your dreams I am pouring the wine
I know I am just a little younger
But my heart feels a little stronger

I don't think it's a crime
To give me some of your time
You are a hand
Of a needed man

I don't want to wait for years
While my face is red from tears
I know you may be very upset
But I am willing to take that step
You say it won't last long
You say I will soon be gone

You feel that I'll lose
You're getting the call house blues

You feel you should pass
But I want it to last
There is no one else
I want you for myself
The voice of softness
Please stop this madness
I don't want none
I want this one
Can't you see how it's been
I do not want to lose again
I tell you while on my knees
Babe I need you please

Is love really real
Are you the way I feel
Can't you see my point of view
There is no one else but you

You say you have told me
But I just want you to hold me
You say there is a way for me to lose
You're getting the call house blues

I know I am on my own
With you I am not alone
You want to know when
I'll ever hold you again

My feeling will always grow
For the love will show
You say we will be through
But babe I want to be with you
I'll tell you I won't lose
You want to have the call house blues

Babe I don't want this
To be the very last kiss
I will always know
That I'll never go
So hold my picture
As I kiss your letter
You won't let me lose
With those call house blues

BOUNCE INTO YOUR HEART

I'm trying to
But I just don't know how to
Yet I am showing you what I can do
Taking that step with the ball in my hand
Letting you step in
Giving you a chance even tho you might not be
That person on my team
I try to be kind as I step out of line
I want you in the touch of my bounce
As I try to take it giving every ounce

Holding may be hard at first to do
It's what I need as I throw the ball
Making it in the hoop
Seeing your smile and calling my name
You showing up at the game
As you aim and click
Bounce into your heart
I think I've got as the clock ticks
Dribbling the ball in my left hand

If I don't make the shot
Still give me that look
Whether we win or lose
I'm going to keep on trying
To bounce into your heart
Because you gave me that start
My motions are going through my mind
Putting your hand on my back each time
Trying to be a coach and friend

I'm here to do my part
Bounce into your heart

BATTERY

Red ruby on positive +
Black leather on negative – I want silk
Brown curl cord hair
Brown plug eyes
If you handle with care
With one big surprise

Under this old cold hood it's me
Not sharp as a box but curvy
Now will you come here and see
I need a good charge from you
Don't want to run out of energy
Not just a jump will do

Don't forget the spark plugs now
You and I will meet and touch ground
I don't need a service guy
I want to met eye to eye

Now I can turn on the radio
And touch you like so
We don't need very much money
Keep on charging me, honey
I need all the warranty
Just like a battery with a lifetime guarantee

ALL I DID WAS WAKE HER UP

Everyone loves her soft voice
She always gives you a choice
All I did was wake her up
Listen to all her stuff

Now she's no longer kissing butt
She knows where she's at
Now I say what a kiss
Now she sleeps peaceful right
Next to me

All I did was wake her up
Listen to all her stuff
Now she's no longer kissing butt
She knows where she's at
Home sweet home

AT EASE

My mind was at ease with you
I notice your point of view
I found myself very confused
And how we were both used

The hours we had
The times I was mad
You brought me a smile
That lasted a long while

You seem a lot that way
I wanted to stay
The night was young
But we have just begun

A friendship I'd like to keep
Our feeling so very deep
Of who we might meet
If you need me I repeat

I am at ease with you
I like what you do
You're much like me
And I like what I see

So when you need someone
You know the job won't be done
Until you buy me a drink
And we sit down and think

For I am at ease with you
And all the things you do
For we are the same
And we care for life's little games

I am at ease with you

A GAY GUY HOLDING MY HAND

A gay guy holding my hand
I thought he was crazy
Right then, right then he took my hand
Serious and not lazy

He told me he wasn't going to be straight
But he still needed a date
I kissed a gay guy, tell me why I still say hi
I dated him for a year
And now he has no fear

He said He "needed to be free"
Just let him be
He looks at guys
The way I do, it's crazy
He talks like me, it's funny

I can't believe I used to make out with him
He said, "Turn me loose"
I need the juice
I 'm ready for him

I gave him some space
I am competing with the human race
How can you be born with it
Now I have a girlfriend who is a lesbian I met
And my boyfriend is with him
Yet they are still my friends
Now that I've met a guy that is my kind

July 25, 2008

RECEIVING IS BELIEVING

I am willing to give
Are you ready to receive
Just to look at me

I want to feel good
With a friend online
Just someone to talk too
It feels so sweet to hear your voice

You don't have to give your number
To receive some kindness from me
Now you and I have a friend
Someone we can give a hand or hug

You just cared for someone
You don't even know
You've told them they've both been good
They have a friend to believe in

I am here online just to talk to
Not take your number
To hear if things are okay
To be a friend
Receiving is believing
With me

November 30, 2008

I WANTA TOUCH ON

I wanta touch on
You and me move along
Wanting to believe
I wanta feel your relief

Trying and trying to get by
Wanting to understand might
Not knowing each other's heart
Yet wanting still to be a part

You've known this person forever
Now you're whoever
Just feeling the pain
Touch still going insane

I wanta touch on
Love and go on
Wanting to belong
Feel our love still being strong

Need to be depth with you
What I can we start to do
Will we end
Or being
Help on to you my friend

Saying no to you
Wanting love too
Pushing myself back
Trying to stay on track

I feel my life is trapped
I wanta touch on
Let me feel like I belong

Help on help on
I wanta touch on
Don't leave me alone
Hurry home
I wanta touch, touch on

July 8, 2009

PORTRAIT OF A TEENAGER'S DREAM

I was just a lonely girl
In a nothing place it seems
It was only in my dreams
You were there by my side
Helping me through the lonely nights

The girls would pit their
Soul in hopes to the love they
Never knew
Just to find someone like you

The portrait of a teenager
Was lost when I was seventeen
But I always thought that
Love was about falling in
And dropping out

So easily, so easily

That is when you took me in
A teenager dream will now begin

With you, with you

The portrait of my teenager dream

The girls would pit their
Soul in hopes to the love they
Never knew
Just to find someone like you

So easily, so easily

A BLINK OF AN EYE

It was the month of October
When a blink of an eye took over
Yet the months went by
Before we had a chance to say hi

It took a year to know
That I could care for you so
I still remember that day
Now I feel you should stay

In the darkness of December
I will always remember
Just because of you that night
Somehow everything turned out right

Never forgetting the blink of an eye
I felt love and now I know why
For our hearts met at both ends
And I am glad we are friends

Lips felt the softness
The beauty became a weakness
For in one enjoyable night
Somehow it turned out so right

It was the month of October
When a blink of an eye
In the darkness of December
I will always remember
With just a blink of an eye
I felt love and now I know why
For some reason it's hard to say
GOODBYE

15 DAYS AND LOVING EVERY MINUTE

15 days and loving every minute of it
Don't hunt me down
It's just hell without it
Nice to be here, but I need
Somebody ... wait, why me

Just like a concentration camp
We all have one own addiction
Where the hell is she too
Right in front of you

13 days and loving every minute of it
Somebody sitting out my window
This is real good for my system
Just be good to me I'll get
Better in a couple of days

9 days and loving every minute of it
Not having a fit
Just excuse the mess
Thanks, wow, I have success
5 days and loving every minute of it
Guess that they let me out early

A BLAZING SUN

I remember a friend
She was a lot like you
I touch her rough skin
Inside the hurt was no end

She let out her tears
Telling me about those years
Love was never there
No one had time to care
She would hit the wall
She felt the tears shouldn't fall

She wanted to prove to the world that
She was like any other girl and knew
Where it was at

She told me
You got feeling
You can help the willing
She said
You believe in me and now even
Though I am blind I can see

I said day and night I am here
Sunlight and moonlight I will care
I am here, love has begun
This is no longer a blazing sun

10 A.M.

I wake up at 10 a.m. with the radio on
I can see that you are not here
So quietly you tiptoe on the floor
A silence of closing that door

I wondered when you will be here again
Why do you leave, you never say why
I wait and wait then soon you slip back
Into my life
Then everything seems so nice

Then that next morning you're gone again
You bring me dreams of roes and a loving heart
But as soon as it's 10 it ends
And everything seems to fall apart

Everything became silently
Everything happens so quietly
I don't know where to go or what to do
All I do is think of you

Until the day you slip back in
The footsteps never hear of
As you go silently again
What's gone, you my love

Since 10 a.m., since 10 a.m.

Could you just stop closing that door
So quietly putting your toes on the floor
And just stay here by the side of me
Wake up with the radio on and let
Everything be with just me
What is gone
You my love
Since 10 a.m., since 10 a.m.

Oh oh oh oh oh oh oh oh oh oh

MELT WITH YOU
THERE'S NOTHING I WOULDN'T DO

You know so many times I
May forget you're mine
But you're always on my mind
There's not time when I am
Without you

I have you right here even there
You are with me everywhere
So don't stop wherever you go
I want you to know

Melt with you
There's nothing I wouldn't do
Come on stop, slow down
Let's get out of here
I want to show you
How you feel to me
So soft
Got to get away

You're always here even there
Melt with you
There's nothing I wouldn't do
I wouldn't do, with you

A GOODBYE TO YOU AND I

While I sit here by the window
I hear your voice very low
It seems so very hard to turn me off
Your voice was nice and soft

While I sit here waiting for you
I wonder why you do the things you do
The one and only guy
I wish I knew why

Hold me tightly and never let me go
Hold me tonight the only way you will know
For you I need to be by
For you I can hold on to the sky
For every little bit of you and I

Allan there's no other guy like you
Even those you didn't show I feel for you
I guess I will never know why
I guess this wasn't for you and I
Just a few words of goodbye

I have tears in my eyes
Deep inside I want to know why
You were so very soft
How come you turn me off

Now I know there is no chance
To see my new romance
I can feel it saying goodbye
Yes a goodbye to you and I
Just a few words of goodbye

OUR LIFE SPEEDS BY ME

Our life speeds by me
I hear the sound near me
Looking as I'm hoping to see
Are you still a part of me
Our life speeds by me
Once again am I free

Am I free, am I free
Getting closer to my destiny
From you the touch is gone
Yet I'm still hungry and strong
Wanting deep inside to belong

My heart became a pumping beat
As the air fills my lungs' streams
I flow more with the wind into you again
But, now as a friend, holding on till the end

Our children need us now
Closing tightly as they learn how
Keeping our souls together with a prow
Do we know what to do, tell me how

We had a head start
Then we fell apart
Now where are our hearts
With our children smarts
Still falling apart and getting older
Who's colder
Our life speeds by me
In our kids' eyes
Once again I'm free
Our life speeds by me
You will never let me be
But our kids will soon set me free
From you, from you, it always comes back to me
Let's take care of our children, leave me be
I'm free, I'm free, can I be me

To Randy Jones
May 27, 2009

IN THE LIGHT OF SHAWN'S EYES

In the light of Shawn's eyes
You are a hero in disguise
So get off your feet
Later hold onto the sheets
After you rush to her heat
To stop and slow meet
Because she's doing the dance
That you want to repeat
She's felt you inside down deep

Giving you the chance of a golden light
You will make it through the night
Her family is holding on tight
Hoping you all will be alright

March 14, 2009

IN MY EMPTY GUITAR CASE

I see a jealous face
Fingers touch the strings
Among other things
I race while I play in space

Hearing notes in a quiet case
My words take the place
Wanting so much to hear
The sound in my car
I put the guitar aside
Leaving pen and paper inside

Only played one song in my life
I became strife to that girl
Being to travel in the world
I took a pen and wrote in my world

Still having a beat
My words became the heat
Yet I still race
When I take out my guitar case
I still see the jealous face
As I play in space

March 25, 2009

DON'T BE A FOOL OVER A STUPID GUY

He will never try
Just hurt you and lie
Don't be a fool over a stupid guy
Reaching out only to cry

Giving your all until you fall
Believing in him again and again
Seeing the pain rush through your veins
Don't be a fool over him
Stop, listen, and think
Tears fall in the sink

A mirror of your face
You feel so out of place
Caring so much
Feeling that touch

Then he is up and gone
You wonder what you did wrong
Wanting so much to belong
Somehow you get up on your feet and walk on

Don't be a fool over a stupid guy
He will never try
Just hurt you and lie
Leaving you behind with one more tear in your eye

June 29, 2009

GIVE ME YOUR MYSPACE

Give me your MySpace
As I sit on your laptop opening my Facebook
And I will be your Gmail girl
Showing you all my photos
Just to turn, turn you on
As you blog me so hot in your words
Later picking me up in your Thunderbird

Now my body is all Googling over you
I hear the words from your Yahoo.com
Giving me Hotmail and texting me hard
Wanting me to waste my minutes and call
No more going online to browse
Being aroused
4playing is just a touch button away
Hitting me with that head shot pic
Baby you've got my download
As you go upload into my iTunes
Now I have a MyFoxSpokane.com

Give me your MySpace
As I sit on your laptop opening my Facebook
And I will be your Gmail girl
Just to turn, turn you on
As you blog me so hot in your words
Later picking me up in your Thunderbird

August 18, 2009

I USED TO KNOW

I used to know this girl
So very well
Even though were I still
She's still in my underwear

Even though she's doing me
She swears up and down
She don't care
But she's got me from the inside out
She tells everybody, what's it all about

I'm still smoking and drinking a beer
Feeling it right in here
I know the baby's coming near
Am I ready for another
She's always been my lover
Yet life's been touch and go
I just don't know
I don't know

I take it one day at a time
Hoping not to lose my mind
I used to know this girl
So very well
But now I just don't know
I don't know
But I want her and this baby even sooooooooo

To Bill
May 28, 2009

SKIN TO SKIN

It used to be skin to skin
But that was back when
When we had love and more
But that was before

I wish we could be one again
By the touch of your hand
Tracing my face with your fingers
Stare into your deep blue eyes no longer

Skin to skin
I won't forget your touch
Still wanting you so much
Now you are gone
With another one

Skin to skin
That was back then
Being far away from one another
Wishing once again to be together

Once again, all I ask
Let me be skin to skin
Making it last
Trying hard to forget the
Love of you and the past

May 13, 1987

TUCK ME IN

Tuck me in under the covers
Over and over be my only lover
Beside my pillow you're my man
Holding you with the sheets close again

Tuck me in
On the phone tonight
Saying those words make it right
In my ear, I'm hearing
So softly I'm feeling

Tuck me in, tuck me in
Can't sleep alone again
Don't want to be alone
Your picture in and by my phone

Feeling the covers loving you
Babe I know, I know it's true
Close my eyes I'm going under
Feeling the magic words
In the dark under no longer

Wherever you are
As you drive off in your car
I know, I know you are not far
Tuck me in again and again
Feeling the covers lovin' you
Babe I know, I know it's true

Tuck me in under the covers
Over and over be my only lover
Feeling the magic words
In the dark as I go under
You're mine forever
Tuck me in, tuck me in

February 23, 2009

RUNNING DOWN MY SIDE

Adrenalin running down my side
Into my soul wanting you to hold
As I fall out of control
Not feeling nothing
As my heart pumpin' something
I'm not too old, chills of cold

Yet I'm scared of death reaching me
Not ready for my illness to let me be
Pulling my skin across the wind
Tying my veins, holding my blood thin

Flushing in and out just to survive
Hoping for a kidney to stay alive
Running down my side
Into my soul, I fall out of control
Feeling proud and bold

Not feeling nothing
As my heart pumpin' something
I am a man
In danger is who I am

Yet I'm scared of death reaching me
Not ready for my illness to let me be
Pulling my skin across the wind
Tying my veins, holding my blood thin

Adrenaline running down my side
Into my soul, wanting you to hold
Still out of control
Chill of cold …

To Mike
April 18, 2010

SUCKING UP THE HEAT

You're always on the go
Not stopping you know
Sucking up the heat
Falling off your seat

Taking too many sips
As I move my hips
Trying to stay clear
Of every word I hear

Sucking up the heat
Tell me so, how sweet
Getting closer and closer
Don't burn me like a toaster

Hand check me
Now on your feet, free
Sucking up the heat
Falling off your seat
I feel you leaping
As we are meeting
Leap, leap, again
Sucking up the heat
I'm feeling your leap

February 28, 2009

I KNOW YOU'RE SUCH A YOUNG TOY

I know such a young toy
But I like pretty boys
Pulling your jacket off
On the dance floor
Hearing your friends breathe
You want more

Showing me what you've got
Maybe not, maybe not
Licking your lips
Reaching for that kiss

Your leg goes between
As I bend over to lean
Hearing your friend say
Get it on with her
I know you're such a young toy
But I like pretty boys
Oh, oh, young toy
Oh, oh, come here boy

February 28, 2009

HE SAID WHERE IS SHE AT

He said where is she at
I said right in front of you
Are you sure you know what to do
My boyfriend said where is that
I just walked up and walked away
He said what does she got
I said I will show you her
Turned and walked away
Now he's off finding her
She is way up there
Hey where is your best friend
What, come again
Don't go, I want to know
Where is she, right over here
Okay I'm on it
And now he's loving it
I just taught him a lesson
And he isn't touching
I'm climbing, I have his loving
And now we have children
He is going to make it
So don't have a fit
If it doesn't fit
She's right in front of you
Taking our first step
Now you can dance and walk away
Look at the others but get your stuff and go
Now at the Dollar Store
Over in Hollywood getting a movie
That she made
This is where she's at

FRIENDSHIP LOVE

First we were two people
Knew each other very little
She had you
I met someone too
The friendship will stay together
No matter, wherever
Tears you saw in my eyes
But you never would cry
Friendship love is it
Friendship love could be a hit
Now all of a sudden we're one
The fights we had are done and gone
Friendship love I am scared
You say you fought and dared
But the Lord says yes
Maybe it was for the best
Friendship love I feel it
It's making me have a fit
We are taking it slow
But somehow I just don't know
We see the stars together
And dance without music forever
As the time goes by
So do you and I
Friendship love
Who are you thinking of
You say you don't want to lose me
And you will always be there
So I just sit back and watch it be
But somehow I have this great fear
See
But some day I feel you want to be near
Not even to say I am here

DREAMTIME WASTED

Just tears in my eyes
As I hear the lies
Working so hard at night
Putting it in writing right
Dreamtime wasted
Copy and then pasting

Try to put the words in
Holding up my chin
Feeling the tears again
Alone at the very end

Who, who will believe in me
Who, who will actually see
As my words run free
I can feel what I wanta be

Dreamtime wasted
Who will reposted
Up at night till daylight
Trying to spell while
I am in hell
Got to get it out before I shout
I am signing out

March 5, 2009

GRANDMA TROT

This is how my grandma
Makes it up the stairs
She does the grandma trot
And then pushes the Walmart cart

She goes through day by day
Making her way
Getting up and dressing
Doing the grandma trot
She goes back up those stairs

She has friends and family
With her grandkids
She dances the trot
She just doesn't stop

But she does take a break
At McDonald's
She loves to eat there
Her children and grandkids
Drink water on the rocks
Putting on their socks

Let's do the
Grandma trot

December 5, 2008

BOXERS WITH RED, RED KISSES

Boxers with red, red kisses
Under my black silk skirt
Covering it up add a red shirt
Dancing around the floor
Them not knowing what's in store
Passing chocolate kisses to the guys
Giving heart lollipops to the girls

Hearing each word in the song
Every beat comes along
Moving so sexy with the girls
Dance touching with the guys
Going in and coming outside then in again
Trying to find him before the end
It's so close to that time
Wanting to have a valentine
Closing my eyes wishing you were mine

Giving her my only rose
Up in the cage we go
Boxers with red, red kisses
Now he can see I have a misses

Hearing the screaming with the song
As my skirt goes up seeing boxers
With red, red kisses
The song ends smiling alone
You appear on your own
Dinner for two
At 2 a.m. with you

February 15, 2009

BLACK LACE

Right through the back lace
I reach out to touch your face
Leather seems everywhere
I wanted skin to touch here

What happened to our touch
Skin on skin wanting so much
I try to pull off the leather
But we are so far from each other

Tears fall wanting you
How am I going to get through
The way you used to make me feel
I live for your love so real

I reach out through the black lace
Wanting so much to touch your face
I feel the leather once again
Far against my body
That used to feel so lovely

I want to have so much again
I'm reaching for what I had then
Through all the leather and black lace
I am waiting to touch your skin, your face

To Royce Hopkin
January 13, 1988

CLINGING ON TO THE HOLD THAT COULDN'T LET GO

I hear all I feel inside
Dying as I cry, seeing you in my eye
Are they our lies one more time
Still wanting you to be mine
I reach only to hear
Our truth in the end
Pain still there again and again

Unsure to hear every word
Then you and I swear and dare
As you hold on tight
I stay awake in pain
Seeing you in the night

Wanting to forget and forgive
Not hearing from you the words
How sorry, how sorry, you are
Trying to show you I can make it better
I can make it right, we can sleep tonight
Finding out that we both are wrong
Trying to pick up the pieces and be strong
Knowing we both are hurting, feeling alone
Running in circles, are we on our own

Trying to rest, giving each other a test
Losing in tears, holding as tight
Seeing only tears, feeling the fears
Still reaching out to make it right

Wanting to sleep in peace
Not able to close our eyes
Looking out the other side
I feel all I hear
Dying as I cry, now hearing sorry
Yet I still worry

Taking a break from one another
Still feeling the ache in each other
Trying not to call
Wondering where you are
Saying it's not you
What else can we do
Leaving each other alone
Hoping to find inside home
Hoping the dying will go away
Being able to feel the love
Someday

I hear all I feel
Dying as I cry, seeing you in my eye
Just to hold you one more time
I want to ease the pain in your body and mine
My son, my son
Trying to forget, trying to forgive
Was I wrong, were you wrong
Trying to keep you safe
Was all I was doing
Tears keep on falling

I shouldn't have, I should have,
Yet I'm still dying inside
As I let you go each time
Touching the bruises in our hearts
As you and I fall deeply apart
My son, my son, hold on to me
Let's rest as we set each other free
Clinging on to the hold
That couldn't let go

To my son Kyle at 18th
Love Mom and Grandma
Beau and Savannah
May 24, 2009

IS MY NUMBER REALLY UP

Is my number really up
Is my number really up
He said to me "cough it up"
But I looked at him up and down

Walked up to him and turned around
He said nothing more than the five words
Before
"I was talking to you" after 26 years as I do

Is my number really up
Who's that girl on top
Is my number really up
He said "you'll always be my naked top"

I never looked at another guy
Cheated never or said goodbye
But I feel I'm not on top
Is my number really up

Is my number really up
Is my number really up

WANT SOME DAMN LOVIN'

Want some damn lovin'
Stop the burnin' inside
My mind racing on by
I'm not going to hide
Inside deeply, deeply crying
Why you're lying

The dark side traveling on
Giving me some before, before I'm gone
Slowly cooking me on high
Why I reach out and lie
I just want to be in your mole
Don't rush me into that hole
Stop telling me why
Inside deeply, deeply I die

Want some damn lovin'
In my life
I'm still coming
Beside that heated knife
Put that arrow in my heart
Never to fall apart

February 23, 2009

IN A DOUBLEWIDE

I don't know why I lied
But he was too busy otherwise
Making love in a doublewide
Later tears hit my eyes

Crying about it as I run and hide
You rushing to my side
Let's clean up the doublewide
Before you say goodbye

Seeing Mary again
I knew we were through
I stop because I love him
More than you

Yet, he's out doing it too
What to do, what to do
Come on step back in
Just being your close friend

ON THE EASTSIDE

I love you on the eastside
Never the north I hide
Come on over to the eastside
Not the south where I lie
Later we can do it on the wild west
Then I can rest

Not uptown or down
On the eastside I'm found
Put me back on the ground
We can make it all year round

On the eastside
I'm your girl
Gimme, gimme your world
Before I die

I love you on the eastside
Never the north I hide
Come on over to the eastside
Not the south I lie
Later we can do it on the wild west
Then I can rest

On the eastside
I'm your girl
Gimme, gimme your world
Before I die

On the eastside

October 3, 2009

THIS IS THE BUS FOR ME

This is the bus for me
I'm on 73
Even though it takes frequent stops
I get off at one hop

I make it to my destination, to you
It's just a good arrangement, to say I do
I like it when you say hi
Before you say goodbye
The smell of your hair
Your love is always there

Just a bus stop
And I'm off
In one hop

Hardly no bills to pay
I just make it slow on my way
Getting closer by the day
Such a little bit to pay
Yet I want you to stay

This is the bus for me
I'm on 73
Even though it takes frequent stops
I get off at one hop
Here is my stop
And my last hop

March 5, 2009

I WASN'T SUPPOSED TO

I know I wasn't supposed to
But I did
I shouldn't have
You told me just this once
But last night we did it twice
I wasn't supposed to, it isn't right
But you're still in my arms tonight

Making a mistake
I didn't hesitate
Yet you felt it
And still melted
You and I were in it
And you so innocent

I wasn't supposed to
But I did
You said you felt something missing
As you lay there while we were kissing

I'm on my knee
Wanting to give you the world
Will you marry me
And love our baby girl

I wasn't supposed to
But I did
I shouldn't have
You told me just this once
But last night we did it twice
I wasn't supposed to it isn't right
But you're still in my arms tonight

Our love is so true
As you and I say I do
I wasn't supposed to
But I did

October 3, 2009

BLUE-EYED BABY GIRL

She came to us five months ago
Little did we know
That we would love her so
With a sparkle in her eye
She walked in and we were surprised
Now she runs across the floor
Letting us laugh more and more
Getting into mischief
As she gives me a handkerchief
Blue-eyed baby girl
She's in our little world
Filling us with joy
As she plays with her toys
She tries to say the words
Telling us with her hands
Dancing with the music
She's got some words down
As she jumps off the ground
We love you Brooke
All it took was one look

FISHING FOR MY MEDICATION

Fishing for my medication
In a tackle box with a few hooks
Just a lot of pills in bottles
Of pain trying to stand clear of that hated
Up with water to my weight full of waste
Yet I can't wait for the bait
To catch that salmon taste
I take each empty bottle
Tear off the label
Put a little note of hope
And throw it into the sea
Hoping you're thinking of me
Along with my line one more time
Hooking my way to the bottom
Only to catch myself each time
As I will in the line
Fishing for my medication
I have time and patience
By stopping and taking the last pill
Feeling the waves in my heel
I come home with more than a bite
I made myself hook up just right
Line and sinker
I'm a damn good willin' thinker

March 4, 2009

SHOT DOWN

I was always shot down
Never got on that stage
Just put in the background
Who never got to say a word

Never met the mike
And sing that first word
Felt I never could
Because no one let me
Believe I could sing

So I wrote instead
Every last word
Even those I couldn't spell
A big word

I still got out there
Hoping someone would show
Me the way
I don't want to be scared
But I always had my fears

Not knowing a note
Or pronouncing a word
Doesn't mean you can't
Do anything you're feeling

Give her or him a chance
Soon they will be SINGING
Let them mess up again
Soon they will be
ACTING LIKE A FOOL
AND THAT'S PRETTY COOL

November 27, 2008

WHY CAN'T I FIT IN

Tell me why I can't fit in
Why can't I be your friend
I don't want to act like you
I just want to be with you
Tell me why I can't fit in
Will I ever win
Tell me how can I be friends
Why won't you let me in your fun
You seem to be always on the run
When I walk in

Why can't I be your friend
When will this ever end
You've always got time
When you needed a dime

Why can't I be your friend
I want to know
Tell me why AGAIN

Why can't I be your friend
What can I do that I haven't done
For you
I've tried that too
What can I do so we can be friends
What is there to do to let me in
I will climb the high tree
Just to let you know I am me
I want to be your friend

LET ME PLAY WITH IT HARD

It's in my hands
Let me play with it hard
Here are the cymbals man
Feel the touch
Running through me
Head rush, rush it's such a plus

Hot and sweaty
Just a little leery
Beating my thing
In shades I still sing

Pushing my foot to the ground
Pumping up and down
My stick, my sticks
The redness on my pants hit
A wild bloody fix

Bandage up my hand
I'm still in the band
They call me the drummer
Doing it down under

Let me play with it hard
It's in my hands
Here are the cymbals man
Feel the touch
Running through me
Head rush, rush it's such a plus

October 3, 2009
To The Old Edge, Jimmy the Dogg Davis the Drummer

TAKE THE SHORTS CORNER

Don't go corner to corner
Take the Shorts corner
Give a little of love to the one
Who is stealing her dreams
As she tries to take care of her boys
She tries to keep them together
With hardly a plate of love
Till she met a man, he shows her the way
Helping her get on her feet
And walk this way

She soon had a daughter
But no money to raise her
So she made a wish to find her
As she let her go so young
To a lady that once helped her with her boys
She remembers years later
And asks her to take care of her daughter
She took care of her boys the best she could
Yet she died at a young age
Missing her daughter
Her daughter found the boys
And learns all about her

Now the family became one
Take the Shorts corner
Don't go corner to corner
Love someone who is unfortunate
You will have a rich heart
Never to part
Finding each other love
After all these years of letting tears

HE TOUCH MY TAIL

I used to wear cheap things
Made it in my big jeans
I'm not yet lean
I'm still pretty not mean

He touch my tail
That kinky-size male
Now we both have handles
And we are kissing by candles

Jammin' to the music in big shorts
Check out the baseball court
At the YMCA
In our lean machine
Taking the weight off me and you
You swim in spandex
I in bikini with a white t-shirt on
Getting wet is so much

He touch my tail
That kinky-size male
Putting arms around each other
My hand was right on him
As he touch my tail
Now he's my male

December 8, 2008

MONOGAMOUS

I want to be so true
To me! To you!
Monogamous, monogamous, yes
I need each breath to be your kiss

I want my love to be strong
I just can't be wrong
That face, lips, those eyes
Tell me, I am the man, not some guy

I'm opening up my heart
Tears inside as I fall apart
Showing you more than just my world
You all a beautiful woman, not just some girl

Still keeping that promise each day
Hoping your love and kindness will stay
Monogamous … monogamous, yes
Being a partner to only one
You're no longer a Miss
Don't, don't tell me I'm gone, I'm gone

I want to be so true
To me! To you!
Monogamous, monogamous, yes

COULD THERE BE A REASON WHY

Sometimes I want to cry
But I am not sure the reason why
Teardrops come down from my eyes
How can I say the words goodbye

There are things in my mind
That I just don't understand
I try to put them behind
But they are there still like the back of my hand

Feeling that I never felt before
I can't help but try to score
Looking on when they say no
God! It really hurts even so

Sometimes I want to cry
Could there be a reason why
Looking into your eyes
I am going to have to say goodbye

The feeling that I felt
Will never ever melt
But I must go on
Even now I could be wrong

There are still things on my mind
That I must try to understand
And I know they won't leave me behind
They will be there like the back of my hand

Could there be a reason why
Come on now, it is inside
Could you tell me why
Before I say the last goodbye

2 A.M. KISS AT THE LIGHT

2 a.m. kiss at the light
I remember so well that night
The car went through a red light
We heard a crash that night

Everything was so bright
Trying to help, we pull them out
Doing all we can
Helping a woman, girl, and man

Just in time before it blew
Giving mouth-to-mouth to who
Little girl watching out calling out my name
Finding out her father has the same

They all survive
Because you and I were there
I am so glad they're alive
Strangers and still we care

2 a.m. kiss at the light
I want to get that out

When I was 21 with Jay Cupit

I DID IT WITH MY DAD TWICE

I did it with my dad twice
In my wedding dress
Looking really nice
He walked me down the aisle
With tears and a smile

He told me to hold my head up high
As I wiped my eyes
He gave me away to the same guy
Not once but twice
He said I will be alright
Looking into my husband's eyes
I said I do twice
On an island and on land
My dad said I would have the sky
He gave me for my honeymoon
As we floated up high
A round balloon of a new start
Hoping the hot air won't break my heart

Saying to my husband this is it
Welcome to paradise
Holding me as I felt the cold ice
In the breeze

We soon landed
My mother helped out saying it's your life
Will have its up and downs
But you will make it back on the ground
Now I am no longer free
In the air I catch myself
3 years later I was with someone else
I really wanted it to work out
I've let out my shout
Moving on I still feel the hot air
I had the sky, the wind in my hair
My heart may be broken
But I'm still hoping

To float back up
With my feet on the ground
Is it enough

February 23, 2009

I DID IT ON MY OWN

I did it on my own
In worn out tennis shoes
Yet I got off the phone and
Took the time to come home
My mom in tears letting me go
Even those she did, I wanted me too
I know she's right, it isn't my time
But I want to prove I can make a dime

I stopped by to get one more pair
I left behind, just to see her face
Letting her and my grandma hold me
Still feeling out of place
As I walk back out that door
She says I can enter back in any time
Believe in my mind hoping I'll be fine
Wearing out my tennis shoes one more time
Getting off the phone
Taking the time to go back home
Just to hold the both of them again

Says this will always be home
Even though I'm on my own
I still catch a ride to school
Do my homework, while looking for that job
Trying not to be a slob

Telling my friend I've got to go
Not charging my phone
Taking the time to see my loved ones
And making my last call
As I give more than my all
There is another pair waiting for me
And I know where

MAKALA, MAKALA

Where oh where are you
Do you have anything to do
Makala, Makala

Let's come out and play
Come out in the sun
Let's get up and run
Bring the toys and let's have fun

Makala, Makala
There you are with your sweet smile
Come and stay with me for awhile
So we can hide and go seek
Nobody will peek
And they won't cheat
Will you walk a straight line
And play with me more sometime

July 26,2008

UP ON SOUTH HILL

Up on South Hill
I'm still
5 foot 2 and sweet
Don't touch until she
Gets to know you
Hoping to date after we meet
Show me you want me, tell me
Just don't stop
Baby come back
I don't want to be your
Midnight snack
I wanta be more than that
Crackerjack in a box
I am the surprise
That you keep and don't put back
Up on South Hill
Now I'm down getting real
Don't let go as you feel
You old hill

February 15, 2009

YOU'RE LUCKY THAT

I have safety features in the house
Now stop playing with that mouse
And get out of your house

Meet me down at the hottest spot
Dine not wine me, then dance with me
Till way past midnight
Saying all the words just right

You're so lucky that
I have safety features in the house
Aren't you glad you met me online
And played with that mouse
I got you out and about

And now you are running around
With your new spouse
Playing house
Doing it in our
Warm sweet home

Trying to keep me down
While I kept you around
Running you into the ground
Lose more than my time
But you keep on calling
With your last line
Says you don't mind

It all starts with that mouse
And my safety features in my house

February 9, 2009

IT'S ... SO ... HARD ... TO ... FORGIVE

Look at me, look at you
So far so near
Yet you know we all care
Things may happen each day
Yet I love you in every way

You give me some space
I run to some place
Sit and think about what to do
Was it my sister's fault or mine, who?
Just meet me halfway
I will do the best I can
I don't know what else to say
Let's take it day by day

It's so hard to forgive
I want to learn how to give
You are my mother
I want to be with you
My sister and my brother
I love you all forever
I want us to be together

July 23, 2008
To the Mason Family

WHO WAS THAT GUY
THAT GAVE ME A WARM HUG ONLINE

Who was that guy
That gave me a warm hug online
I can feel it deep inside
Right between the lines
He so hot, so fine, I want him to be mine
I want to know who, I want to know was it you

Who was that guy between my lines
I'm ready to feel it again and again
I felt the heartbeat
So close I want to meet
I'm out of my seat and up on my feet
On the east side
I'm ready to spread, spread wide
My arms and hold you strong
Hoping you will carry me slowly along
Come down to the east side come this way
Through the line, entering my mind
I want that hug of mine to stay

I can feel the pump in your voice a loving heart
As I touch the blood run through my lower part
Who was that guy
That gave a warm hug online
I can feel it deep inside, right between the lines
Wrap once again as you slap my behind
With you there, nothing to hide
Who was that guy
That gave me a warm hug inside, I'm running back online
Was it you, I think it was you, I want you too
Hug me warm between the lines
Like you do touch mine

3 MAGIC WORDS

Could you say those
3 magic words
Oh my god
Oh my god
You bring the body
I'm really horny
Where are you boy
I'll bring the toy

Oh my god
Oh my god
With me in a
Dark alley
I'm your honey
Meet me with my kitty
And we can get petty
So say those
3 magic words
Oh my god
Oh my god

February 26, 2009

MATH PIECE

You do the math
And I'll give you a piece
Here's the receipt
Now there's time under the sheets

You always hand me the bill
Touch and feel
First dinner then dessert
Now we are at a resort

Is this the way it's going to be
For you and me
Plays, movies, dancing, on and on
Steamy nights, I want to belong

I've done the math
Let's hit those sheets
Follow the path
Of love in one piece

October 22, 2008

MOM
IN MY HEART

Oh where, oh where
Oh where, oh where
Is my mom
Somewhere, somewhere out there
I know she's trying to get here, she cares
I had her close to us
So close she can see us now
She has a broken heart
When we are so far apart
Oh where, oh where can she be
I'm so helpless but I know
She's coming for him and me
No time to waste, I'm out of place
Can't let her inside go
We need her so, love is in the air
I know you are already here
I'm running out the door and
My brother is running after
I told you, I told you,
Mom are we going back home
No she said, my eyes looked scared

She said our home is now here
I'll find a way so your dad and I
Can be with you both I am getting a home here
We both want you two in our lives, we care
She's here, she's here and she's staying
Where, there, no here
We don't have to change schools
And fly back and forth no more
Mom and Dad live around the corner
From each other and going to each other
Even though they are no longer
We are with our parents because of our mother
I run to her and so does my brother just to show her
Now our older brother is here and we are making it again

By Shawn Jones and family
February 9, 2009

DRIP, DRIP, OFF MY LIP

Drip, drip, off my lip
Put it on my chest
Let me feel your heart
Through my hands
Come on man

This is your girl
Jumping into your world
As long as it takes
Don't break, break
Our love
Pushing hard above
Pulling you in the right spot
I know you're hot, hot,

I'm in it
Keep on giving it
That drip, drip,
Off my lip
Onto my chest
Don't rest, don't rest

Drip, drip off my lip
Onto my chest
Don't rest
As I tip my hip
Playing hard to get
I'm taking the last sip

Drip, drip, off my lip
Onto my chest
Don't rest
As I tip my hip

FIVE ALIVE

I met a man who needed a five
I said I have a five
He said I'll take that five
I told him if he took that five
He had to keep us alive

My number is inside
He asked me for my name
He said there's no number in it
I said get to know me
We began to talk
Then we started to walk

We began to dance
We gave each other a chance
Now my number is inside
Our moments became days
Our love is alive

I still have your five
I am going to keep us alive
With your number inside
Our love is no lie

Five alive
Number inside
Nothing to hide
Keep that five

THE WORLD KEEPS ON CHANGING

The world keeps on changing
None stop planning
Still jumping and showing
We keep on getting up and doing
Making it through the day winning
Or are we sitting here losing

We've gone from white
To black as night
Women are still fighting
Who's wrong trying to get our left out
Quieting our pain and still hiding the right
So when you go from white to black
And hit mankind like that
The world is full of colors
No matter who you are what's a color
To me we are each a star
Just take the time to believe
After all you are someone like me
Red, white, and just a little bit blue
Yet you as people still knowing what to do

Are we working together
Or are we losing one another
As we try to get up high into this world
We were born by just a girl
Why is there such a thing call war
Fighting hard to get there in a truck not car
Yet I care, the new kids in a taxi mama van

Yes we are like animals somewhat wild
But don't you love our smiles
It's time to come home to sweet home
Stop hurting and being alone
Yes you can make it hard on your own
You need to care about the unknown
Going way out into space
Do we still have plans for the human race
I'm not going to reach out and stop
I'm here to stand tall and take that very small shot
The world keeps on changing
I'm still here just planning

March 13, 2009

HE'S NOT YOURS

Half the time
I kiss a gay guy man
He said (you don't know who I am)
He stepped in saying (he's not yours half the time)
(he's mine, all mine, all mine...)

Walking through the mist
The moonlight hit
Seeing him with him like this
In passion they kiss

He's not yours half the time
He's mine, all mine, all mine...

Pointing his finger at me
Saying can't you see
Then swing it back
(my man back on track
Don't touch him like that
It's his last act)

Rain starts to fall down
As tears hit the ground
I know he's right
He's with him tonight
He's not yours half the time
He's mine, all mine, all mine...

April 8, 2010

THE COURT IN OUR WHITE HOUSE

The court in our white house
Giving the children and spouses
Your net
Making each chance
Yours and ours hoops
As we play life with world ball
Giving the peace in our bounce
With every last ounce

Hoping not to move as we fall
Defense not to hurt all
Keeping focus with both teams
Safely as we try
Keeping our closest eyes
Winning or losing we are the U.S.A. team
Standing and running to the basket
With a leap
Hits our tennis shoes, feet
Giving hope to all
With your court ball

SEXY COLORS REALLY MATTER

I want him dark
In the White House to start
Holding as he lets go the troops
I can see the GIs take off their boots

Sexy colors really matter
Bring out the smart guys
Give me the sweet life
With you I will melt
As I turn to the Vice
To hear her explain twice

Color is more than that
You need to follow the path
Get on the crazy track
Find out the sweet facts
As you put it in my pack

Being a president takes time
Are you ready to lose your mind
Doing all you can
Will you win or lose again
Not to be on his back
Never hear the please
As I bend over backwards
Trying to go forward
Am I white or black or Oh mama
Let's get going with Obama

November 10, 2008

COFFEE, TEA, COME FLY WITH ME UNITED AIRLINES

Hello, can I take you to your seat
What, F26, right this way
Coffee, tea, what do you need
You will be there in awhile

Light is on, do you need a blanket or pillow
Yes, a magazine, and how long will it be
Your light was on, do you want earplugs
What's the movie for today, please

Please rinse out her child's bottle
Not a care in the air
Yes, I rang again to get your name
I felt like I was in first-class
We are here at last

We are getting married today
We met on the airplane
Coffee, tea, come fly with me
I met Michael Jackson that day
And we flew away into the sky
Sky's the limit to love

ALOHA

Imagine me wearing a lea and you with sunglasses on
Me dressed in a bikini with a grass skirt almost gone
Nice tan with a flower in my hair
Bare feet in the sand I'm there

So how about a date
In paradise with you as the mate
Surfboarding on the wave
Aloha with a hand is more than you gave

Laying on a towel under palm trees music you played
Me dancing as a hula girl I stayed
Cola nuts we cracked milk we drink
Are we going to be there I think

Pineapple I bite from your lips
Then we touch and kiss
Aloha, aloha, I want to be there
Instead of being here
With you I'm free
Come and be with me
      Aloha

August 22,2008

THE LAST KENNEDY TO GO

Each one trying to be
A part of the White House
Especially my brothers and me
The words were spoken from our mouth

Brother after brother
We followed our father
Helping one another
Respecting our mother

Politics was our life
As we sailed and rising right
Becoming the last Kennedy to go
Shaking your hand strong so

We meant every word to go on
Putting your step along
The Kennedys will carry on

Our lives are ahead
Our words are not dead
Giving all we could
The Kennedys felt they should

The last Kennedy to go
I don't think it's so
We are not alone

By Adella Jackson
September 22, 2009

TWIN TOWERS

It happened one day
In the light of September
This is how it was made
A few men got in a plane
And said a prayer
As they flew up in the air

They got up to take control
They were on a roll
We were fighting for our life
The plane was turned and hit
Right to the twin towers
With all its might
It hit right on sight

People trying to survive
While others stayed alive
One by one the young
Men, women and children die
With no gun

Now 9/11 came about
As they all shout
The towers fell down
People underground
Rushing and panting
Falling and crying
Each person slowly dying

The firefighters and police
And helper could feel their heart beat
In all the heat running in the street
A day no one will not forget
A light of a moment that hit
Never to say goodbye to this date and year
9/11/2001 in tears of all the fears
Pain hit Washington, D.C., Pentagon
And in rural Shanksville was the 4th plane
People were going insane
Losing their minds
All because of these hijackers on the planes
Now we are at war
From afar
Saving the U.S.A. each day

ROLLING UP ONTO SHORE

Our fleet's in the sand still rolling up on the sand
A half bottle of Corona in one of our hands
Getting deeper as I twist off and loosen my pants
Yet I feel shorter each time I look into a man's eyes
Running and dropping no time for stopping
Leaving them behind with tears in both eyes
Ending up back in the sand rolling back
With a machine gun
My heart is still pumping hard on the run

The year was 1967 but I am still rolling
Reaching 1968 hearing my heart break it was all I could take
I was in Vietnam with all the other guys
The mid-day sun beating down my neck
I would tear off my shirt and still bless
Pulling each one across the ground to safety
Holding my friend as I closed my eyes and put them to rest
Saying to myself, can I make it through this

Soon flying in the slick with my helmet tightly on
Hearing the helicopter propellers over my head
As I get to my unit seeing the blood on the wheel
Looking at my partner running to get there

This is done each day and night
Yet I am retired and now old and gray
I hear and feel the sound
We all were awarded but my boots still hit the ground
Now all alone at home I still close my eyes
Feeling the pain down deeper inside
Rolling up on to shore
I try not to bless any more
Just let me rest

To Roger Farrel
February 16, 2009

THE WRONG THAT
COULD HAVE BEEN RIGHT

My father changed this world
While he was in a band being a political man
He met this white girl
She began to care
He let down his scare
She helped him through his world
He wrote these words
In a book I hold
Says I am in it
Follow the war
He had no bullets in the bar
Hijacked a plane
He still aimed
To Cuba a Black Panther
Leaves his family that was so near
Soon sitting in prison with tears
Later he said goodbye
Holding on to the book he soon died
I was told he married there
While he left us still
The wrong that could have been right
Was as black as the still night
Yet I knew he saw the light

As I closed my eyes and held the book tight
A Cuban boy came up to me as white as he could be
Saying I love your father my dad and I'm white
But he fought for black like me
I'm black as night, I held him
Feeling my dad inside him appear the light
Never to blow out his words
With a book we now both hold
Our colors are no longer dark and cold

To Anthony and Family
February 16, 2009

LADY DIANA

My mom called me from the hotel
She said she died and I was only a mile away
People are crying I can't get through the crowd
My tears fell wishing I was there
We came from all over the world

To say bye to her
Both sons walked away
And return the next day

The queen felt pain too
Charles became blue
Coming together to say goodbye
To you Lady Diana
She was the princess that grew into

        A Lady

October 9, 2009

YOU PROMISED ME A ROLL AND A STONE

Feeling the music
When we met
Tasting the love
On our tongue
Looking at our
Face watching Kiss
At first it was
A roll in the hay
Months went by
Then years
Getting closer was
Our biggest fear

Now you and I have been
together for so long
We both love their songs
No more roll in the hay
You said this is the time
You promised me
A roll and a stone
Now I'm wearing one
Hoping we can rock and roll
With the Stones and Kiss
Forever

REMEMBER MICHAEL

Michael Jackson's main attraction
Was his action
As we look down hearing his words
Seeing his moves
We got all his grooves

By the touch of his glove
We all feel his love
Remember Michael
Feeling the Thriller

As our heart pumps faster
The light hits his soul thereafter
Give tears of joy in the music
Feeling of his motions
Give us all emotions

Remember Michael
Will never be forgotten

June 26, 2009

WITH THE GLOVE

With the glove
He's always been five
His sister given the beat
His brothers started him at age five
Doing A B C, 1 2 3
His turn and his slide
His hat, his glove, it always came alive
Bringing a dream for boys and girls
He is known all over the world
I have a brother with his name
Who flies all over the world
I love the song "Thriller"
He's a dad too
They both hold on to their kids
Both in their hands
But the singer has a glove
And slides across the floor
And does both a turn
Only one sings (Blue Jeans)
Yet they both have a sister with the beat
With a hand and glove
That the public love

For Michael Jackson
December 4, 2008

STILL ENDS UP LIKE A VIRGIN

She started out
Like a virgin
Danced her way into vogue
Sometimes she's bold

Giving a kiss to a young chick
Was onstage in a bed
Walked down the stairs
With all the men, in red and diamonds
She still is glamorous

Now she is older
But she still moves like then
Her dancers fall through the stage
She comes up in a cage

She's been a dancing queen
She did a movie or two
Doing the wild thing
Still ends up like a virgin
And has a body to kill

To Madonna
December 4, 2008

FROM TOP TO BOTTOM
HEADED BACK UP

Starting out young
Singing from the top of her lungs
Trying to be someone
Given that kiss of stardom
She met two men and married twice
Having two children of her own
My son has her autograph and picture
She fell into a depression
Divorced her unsure man
Losing everything trying to prove it all
She fell to the bottom

But she's headed back up
Telling her side of the story in a cup
What was she thinking
While she raced to be with them
Hoping for another chance with her kids
In a crazy world
She still is a dancing and singing girl
Looking for love and happiness
From top to bottom headed back up
Her children float up in a loving cup
Just add cream and sugar
With hugs and love as
She sips back to the top

To Britney Spears
November 27, 2008

LIKE THUNDER

Like thunder my tears
Splash harder
As I leave her for another
What I had I want again

Trying for our hopes as she
Takes me from my ex's wife
Will our children understand
My tears come once again

We all try to be friends
For our kids, while our heart bends
Loving more than us
Like thunder my tears

Splash harder
I've been through hell
But my ex's wife and I still live as
Our children survive

Garth Brooks
December 3, 2008

CARRYING UNDER THE WOOD NOW ON A LOG

The girl that is
Carrying under the wood
Of what she could
As she sees her words
In life she pours no more tears

Carrying under the wood
Now on a log
Floating on with these songs
Jesus helped her take the wheel

She can give us more to feel
Before he cheats again
I just can't live a lie
We all need a learning lesson

Just trying to make it through
As we last with the past
Making our own way

Jesus at the wheel
Can help me give one more feel
I'm touching that wheel
Trying to live on my own
Enjoying her songs through
Me and my children

To Carrie Underwood
December 8, 2008

SAXOPHONE BECAME SEXY CELL PHONE

The man I gave my voice to
He plays music with a
    sexy cell phone
I was pregnant with my fourth child
They asked me if I wanted something
To calm me down
I asked for him and an hour later
My daughter arrived with a smile inside
Kenny G played for me
My daughter Savannah
Now she's a teen and listens to
Kenny Chesney
Writing songs for him
As she rides in the wind ...

October 9, 2009

BILLY RAY

I'm a lot like you but with three on my hands
Running without a man
Doing all I can
With my songs in my empty guitar case
As my mother fights to fill her empty books
All true out the blue
And you've got a Jackson too

October 10, 2009

SHE'S MY TIME AFTER TIME

I dressed like her when I was in London years ago
Felt the wind in my hair as I let time go
Met love in the air and you're right there
Next to the castle you open the gate
Trying not to smile, I held on for awhile

Never wearing a watch, I still saw the time
In my hands as I passed you by
I see her step into the carriage all white of beauty
Him step in with long thin tux of color blackest

People around us time stopped again
The horses nodded as they took that walk
Around the circle of love
Seeing the Queen with hat and gloves
In the air I felt the doves

She's my time after time
Cyndi Lauper I am in London
Dancing around the Abbey
Meeting you with a dream come true
Into the night we dance up the lights
Feeling the ground underneath
Loving you was moments of brief
Back on the train I was soon gone
Memories carry on time after time

November 1, 2009

GOING THROUGH HELL

I watched her life story
Saw what she went through
All to get on in this world
As a singer
The way she was treated just
Because she is a woman and was poor
Now she'd moved up in the world and
Sings like you wouldn't believe
Her voice tells the world that
You can do it
Just a few of her songs that I love
"Too Much Man for a Woman," "Sugar, Sugar"
"Push," "Tina's Prayer"
I say to her "Go girl go"
Tears and all she still got up there and sang her heart out
We love your voice Tina Turner

HIS EYES ARE ON HIS SUNGLASSES

His eyes are on his sunglasses
Moves his fingers
Across the piano floor
People listen for more
He sings his way through
Your heart

Married his only man
His dreams follow a keyboard
Their hearts set and soar
Time and time again
It's more than music
It's a melody that comes
Back to me and them

He just doesn't wear them
His eyes are on his sunglasses
We are in his music
And feel connected with his songs

Loving "Island Girl"
And "Candle in the Wind"
My heart is his friend
Don't let the music
Ever end
   Sir Elton John

MY SON NAMED BEAU

But don't take the girl
He wears his grandfather's watch
And says he's the friend in the song
But he knows every word
In the same way

Went fishing years ago
But with his brother and sister
Not that girl
Yet last year he met this girl
And got kissed behind a tree

His dreams of having a girl
Of his own and
To love in the song
He wants to grow up
Having the same love
Please don't take the girl
Out of his world

To Tim McGraw
November 27, 2008

THINKS HE'S A SINGING RANCHER

Thinks he's a singing rancher
Has a voice
That brings joy
To my daughter

She wants to go see him
In concert
Loves his cowboy hat and his voice
Thinks he's a singing rancher
As he touches our hearts
She becomes a dancer

He says he has to roll on in
A big wheel to the stage floor
Just to hear everybody cheer
His voice comes out of nowhere
To hear every word is right there

Thinks he's a singing rancher
As he touches young girls' hearts
My daughter is now a part
Of a rancher's heart

To Kenny Chesney
By Shawn Jones and daughter Savannah
November 27, 2008

JUST LET ME

Time to please what you see
Don't let me be free
It's been too long
I'm ready to be strong

Just let me ... be yours
Just let me ... be yours
Give it your all
Hey give that call
Let yourself fall

Just say the words, you fool
Just let me, just let me
Play more than pool
My heart wants to rule
Stop feeling warm and uncool

Just let me ... be yours
Just let me ... be yours
You got me soaring
Stop my tears from pouring

Just let me in, I'm yours

To Pink
December 22, 2008

MY OLDEST LISTENS TO HIM

My oldest listens to him
With that song
Bring sexy back
He moves the mouse
As he goes to MySpace
On his laptop

Chatting with the guys
On plenty of fish he tries
Till he finds someone
And becomes number one

Now he has a kiss
A picture like this
I'm bringing sexy back
Keeps himself on track
Now he's found that face

On MySpace no time to race
Giving himself and him a chance
For love and romance
Just two good friends
Bringing sexy back
In his ear coming out to his hand
As he touches his new man
Fingers open a new door
Love reaches him once more

To Justine Timberly
December 5, 2008

WHAT I CAN SHOW YOU

See what I've got
Here I am what's she got
I have more so much more
She is before I'm after
Here's my laughter

What I can show you
Is more than what she can do
You know I'm right
Where are you and me tonight

Go ahead spoil me
Just wanta please me
I don't want your girlfriend
I want her boyfriend

What I can show you
Is more than what she can do
She is before I'm after
Here's my laughter

To Avril Lavigne
December 22, 2008

YES, I'M GOING

I wanted so bad to see you
Just days before I was told there was no more
My grandma's birthday was the same day
My mom got tickets for them too
Because she thought I had tickets already

When I came home and told her
She said you can go and handed them over
Just bring me home a shirt for my mom
I know it was on a school night
Yet it felt all right
I went with my sister
We took their seats
Seeing the big lights
People taking pictures with cell phones mine was dead

It was a night I couldn't forget
I had really no money but my sister did
She said come on as we reach through the line
There was hardly any time
I could see him close up
But he could not see me
My sister got a necklace instead
Nothing in my hand

He came back on
With a voice I wanted to be my own
My time isn"t alone
As I walk out the door she handed me a poster
That is now on my grandma's bedroom wall
I have his DVD in concert (LOVE, PAIN AND CRAZY)
We all love Keith Urban
I got to see him on my grandma's birthday

By Beau Jones
September 14, 2009

NOW MY SON CAN

My dad gave him his first computer
He wasn't sure what to do
He began to ask questions
My dad tried to show him
It was hard to figure out
But he was on it all night

As he got older he
Would tell me to take it in
Then he would say it's still not working right
I would pay more each time
Just to get him online
Now look at his mind

Where has he gone
He said I'll fix it myself
I came home with parts everywhere
I shake my head, he said, don't worry
I got it, mom, this part goes here

Now at 18 he made our books fly
Online and in the sky
Thank Bill Gates
My son Kyle Jones
Who's now turning 19
On his own ...

October 10, 2009

WHOOPI GOLDBERG

Sweet chocolate smile
Given that style
Still going strong
Pushing on and on

Shine into my mind
Given her juicy time
Whoopi Goldberg
Like it should

A grandma now flies
Up, up, into the sky
Now she's been through more states
Than rode on the road

Tears of laughter and joy
She was a kind of coy
Whoopi Goldberg
Does it good
Like it should

November 1, 2009

ROSIE O'DONNELL

I watch her on TV
As she brings out the stars
She said she loves Tommy
Across the screen race her car

The children love her so
Even what's up her sleeve
They won't say no
Her size doesn't seem to matter
She gets better and better

Later on as she heard the news
She had to speak up too
And tell Tommy Cruise
That he was her knight
In high heel shoes
Meds play the blues

I still watch her
Hoping
I'll be there
To sweep Tommy Cruise away

ANDREW AND FERGIE

An old friend wrote me
Asked me to come to London
My mom said go see the world
Enjoy the palace and museum and English country
Flew nine hours and met him
Wheel on the other side
Drive so fast yet I saw everything
Met up with his friends
Went to Ipswich then back to London

I saw chaps, the British men soldiers
It was really remarkable
I got him to smile and went on the train
Stayed in a palace and went to Paris
Learned to say, Oui, oui, monsieur
Stood next to the Eiffel Tower
Went to all the fancy hotels
But most of all I ended up
Seeing Andrew and Fergie get married
I was called "Love" as I crossed the street
Danced and tasted "L" Beer, met a GI
Had a great time there

BETTY BOOP

I see you Betty Boop
Give me a smile and I'll toot
Wind up your skirt
To open shirt
It doesn't hurt
I won't dare to look

I see you Betty Boop
Give me a smile and I'll toot
Your open shirt
And wind up your skirt
I promise I won't look
But like an owl
With my big wide eyes
I'll turn and hoot
Driving slowly by
I'll roll down my window
Hoping you have
That will be the day

SHE DANCES ON IN

Not sure of what's in store
They love her more
She dances on in
Flying colors
Hearing your voice
With lips so moist
She's now with her wife
Does it make it right

Love is where you find it
In a person dream you have it
Girl or boy, man or woman
Woman to woman, man to man
Move to move, word to word
We are who we are
Love makes us strong
So we feel like we belong

She dances on in
With a lady not a man
Can my mom do the table
As we dance I know she's able
Ready to me us with a soft touch
Ellen DeGeneres
The Ellen Show

October 10, 2009

FLYING COLORS

This one passing flying colors
But it's not your color
It's your style
That makes the fans love you

THE EMPTY CART

The empty cart fills
Us with love that we already
Have with our family
So get a little and be
Small with a big heart

FARRAH

One of the three angels
Did well with her hair
She didn't wrangle
Falling slowly through
What else could she do

She ended up falling hard
While laying on air
Cancer became her fall
Losing her hair
She gave it her all

With her son and O'Neal
By her side
We all ask why
She had to die
She'll always be an angel
In our eyes

By Adella Jackson
To Farrah Fawcett
June 26, 2009

WHERE IS INDIANA JONES

Where is Indiana Jones
Unlock the combination pull doors
Open I'm stuck and sinking
See in the dark, my heart is breaking
Gotta get away and run to the park
Dry throat, pumping heart, pay the master
Full moon running through the trees
Feeling the stream inside of me
There you are, now we touch
Hip to hip, off again to the craziness
In the cave spiders everywhere crawling
Jump across the river of wittiness
Landing on the edge of falling rocks
Where is Indiana Jones
I can't make it on my own
Running across the unknown
Just to touch you again
Are you my man, reach out for your hand
Getting to the dash now we have the cash
The fortune of gold, I'm so cold
Grab your hat and let's go
We made it through the dew
And I'm still with you

To Dangers
October 14, 2008

OPRAH

When she walks into the room
Eyes begin to shine
Leaving no one behind
Fills hearts with her mind
She's ours and one of a kind
But she made her own dime

By Adella Jackson
October 11, 2009

HUMPTY BECAME DUMMY

Look at you Humpty
Now you're the dummy
You had a great fall
Losing her and all
Left her behind
Treated her unkind

Now all the king's men
Took her other hand
Soon thereafter
They leave you the last chapter
What should you do my friend
To get her back again
You lose her track
All ready to crack

Now she is on her own
And you're all alone
Get back together
In one piece, fix each other

Look at you Humpty
Now you're the dummy
You had a great fall
Losing her and all
Now and hereafter
Put yourself together
And stay with her once again
Never lose the chapter my friend …

DOROTHY AND TIN MAN

Dorothy met Tin Man and
Had a good time but then she left
For the guy who had no brains

Now she's back on the yellow brick road
To meet a guy who gave a good roar
Just to get to the Oz
And have some magic

Along came the broomstick witch
Of the east and got herself all wet
Then she met up with the fairy
That tapped her shoes three times
Soon she was back home with her
Dog, Toto, loving that Tin Man

I'M THE GINGERBREAD WOMAN

I was just baked at 400 degrees
Out of the oven I'm running
As fast as I can with brown curly hair
Big brown eyes, below my chest candy buttons
Around my fly goes whip-up frosting, follow my
Curves I'm running barefoot
Through the woods, are you the gingerbread man
Can you run as fast as you can
Try to catch me as fast as you can
Have a little piece, a nibble from my neck
So warm running in the wind, catch me again
Nibble my nipples as my buttons come off
Now don't forget the whip-up frosting, start licking
I'm running again, catch me as fast as you can
I'm the gingerbread woman
Can you catch, gingerbread man

DRAKE AND JOSH AND SISTER MEGAN

The two half brothers
That really show their
Love and friendship on the show
With their sister and music
Moving on in
Pulling tricks again
Just to show them each
She can do better

It's kind of like our kids
Brothers and sister
Showing their love
While getting into trouble
Proving they can be themselves
And still have fun with their friends
My children just love the show
Because they feel the same way
They are half brothers
And a sister showing what she can do
They all got it together
And really no one's better
But we have fun with our friends
As we sit down to watch your show
Making each other number one

December 8, 2008

HE STARTED OUT DUMB AND STUPID

I used to show him on TV
I told mom he'd make it big someday
From TV shows to plays and now movies
He became an overnight star

From Barbarino to Greased Lighting
To Saturday Night Fever, Hairspray,
Broken Arrow, I was not surprised
I would get up and dance like him even
Get on the floor I watched him more and more

Now he does his own movies, got married
And flies himself in his own jet
My mom said you can start out stupid
And end up a cupid

I remember one year I met a cupid
One night we saved three people's lives
And it was because we were kissing at the light
Things didn't work out so I went on with my life

But I've seen the world and been a simple girl
Planted my seeds and came back out as me
Fell in and out of love waiting, and waiting
For that star above

November 20, 2008

I HAD A BEACH MCINTYRE TOO

He was away
In Korea he wrote me today
He wanted me to be there
He sent a ticket right away

I met Pierce and Winchester
Colonel Potter and Father
Even Radar and Frank
It was so great

The Korean girls weren't the same
Want to go to America, he didn't
Had a mamasan and papasan
In Korea it was hard work
But I had fun
Up the hill I would run
Bring back rice
We all paid the price

I've been to Japan, Hong Kong, Tokyo
And now Korea too
Danced until the music faded
While he was in the field I played
Camp Stanley
Became MASH
With you

Klinger got early leave
He got to go home not me
Taught English
And didn't speak a word
Yet I did all that I could
I had a beach too
I love being with you
McIntyre

All at Camp Stanley
We would get upon
Our feet
To run and dance in heat

SO YOUNG

So hard to lose
The one you love
So young my son

He was so young
I still weep
You can see it in
My eyes so deep

Feeling him still here
I know he's gone there
He is missed
But still in our heart

Is our family falling apart
Flying through his art
I try to understand him
As he became a young man
So hard to lose
The one you love
So young my son

Torn apart by sadness
Dealing with the madness
John and Kelly try to make it
Saying goodbye to Jett
As they hold on to little Ella

So young my son

September 15, 2009

BEAU OF OUR LIVES

We sat down
I put my hand on my tummy
Soon we will have a baby
What to name him
Watching TV

We both love this show
Saying different names
You and I both come
Up with the same
And just like
Beau of our lives
Our Beau has you and
Me, a brother too, love and hope
Take your beau under the
Mistletoe

FIRST HER SON, NOW HER

She couldn't let go
Taking the meds so
Going down hurting as you know
In tears of death
Now we laid them both to rest

Finding out our baby is mine
Her man was out of line
Remembering holding her
One last time

First her son, now her
I hold our daughter
Seeing the smile in her face
Memories in every place

Being a father to our daughter
My love is growing stronger
My blue-eyed blond
Is here taking a pumping part
I'll promise to give her a fresh start
I hold you both in my heart

Lets her know all about you two
In everything we do
Daniel and Anna Nicole I hold on
Through her strong

September 22, 2009
Daniel and Anna Nicole

SPOKANELESS

Would love to meet him, Tom Hanks
His movies help me feel good inside
From Forrest Gump to Sleepless in Seattle
The Green Mile
We enjoyed them all
Picking out movies to bring home
Just to be with our family
And our sweetheart, maybe a friend or two
We also love these

On Golden Pond, Savannah Smiles, Harry Potter, Flubber,
Toys, High School Musical, Jurassic Park, Spiderman, Jackie
Chan, Mask, Cats & Dogs, Free Willy,
Cars, Ghost Busters, Chipmunks, Lion King, Ice Age,
Garfield, Happy Feet, Robots, Indiana Jones,
Pirates of the Caribbean, and so much in store

Hey kids let's go get a movie or two
We are off to Hollywood in Spokane
Sitting down with you a friend
Popcorn and pop is much cheaper
And you can stop the tape
Then do REW or replay, go ahead and buy it
We've got it on our shelf

December 8, 2008

BACK TO THE FUTURE HITS THE PRESENT

Michael J. Fox returns
With his disease ready to turn and learn
Show how his family is surviving
Now in the year 2008 with faith

The gas going up and down, the future is hitting the ground
A new president and war coping with the poor
Friends being gay and lesbian or bi
Their dreams are still real
Holding on to how they deal and feel

Still putting on his power shoes
Closing his eyes and opening up wide
With his family by his side
Taking his medication
That back-to-the-future drink
Gets him by with the music inside

He used to skateboard and fly
Now he takes his time
Making up his mind
Showing that love and dedication
Here's his medication
With a glass of water on the rocks
Reaching over and putting on his socks
Take that refreshing drink
Close your eyes, it doesn't cost a thing to think
Family comes first as you get out of bed
You are one step ahead before you're dead
Back to the future
Hits the present

Michael J. Fox returns
Ready to turn and learn

The time machine is you on your own
Just a dream from a man
And a woman to show you the way
As she takes your hand

Helping her in every way as she plans
For the future with you
Don't stop those lands
Follow through
Hold on to only her in everything you do

November 19, 2008

BELIEVE IN YOUR HEART

There once was a girl who already had love
But yet she felt so alone and not thought of
She was not really fat or skinny
But around middle sized
She spoke soft words to you
Yet still felt very blue

She had her own dreams, like girls do
To be married and to have children and love like you
As the years went by she grew and grew
Before she knew it time just flew

Boy after boy soon man after man
She fell in love and out again
She would have silent tears
She went on her own facing her fears

She went to the Lord and he said
"Believe in your heart
Remember 'till death do we part"
One day she met two men
She fell in love with one then the other
The first one went far away after a year
The second one was married and had a son

She loved both men
But she felt too young
Now she's with child with the married one,
ask him to get a divorce, to bring her the final papers

From afar weeks went by more and more letters
Received a ticket with love
Flying above to reach his destination
Closed her eyes, made a decision

She went to the Lord and he said
"Believe in your heart
Remember 'till death do we part"

Hoping she was right
She kissed the married man goodnight
Abortion she felt her stomach and went through with it
She went and told him what she had done
She kissed him and his son
Got on a plane and flew to the man from afar
And married him after all

Yet she missed the married one and his son
She no longer has his child inside her
Her wedding was a fairy tale come true
She was with child soon again and out came a son

She loved them both dearly
Working hard for her love ever after
They fought and fought and still lovers
He would always end with flowers
One day soon the marriage ended
She had to bring him the final papers

She went to the Lord and he said
"Believe in your heart
Remember 'till death do we part"
Make amends and still being friends
For the child's sake don't make a break
So she signed the papers and said
"So our baby can see both families"
Later he remarried and had four more

Returning to the scene of the married man
She could not find him yet
She met up with a drunken fool
Put in the paper for a husband with his tools

Fifty-four letters in a box
Combination wishes key to the lock
Invited one into her heart
Found her soul mate
Believing in her heart
'Till death do we part

Finding out she spoke with soft words
Of a child that wasn't his
Abortion again she thought was so hard
Apart with her own hoping to never be alone

Soul mate wished to marry her
Crossed her fingers another child grew
Seven months later married the soul mate
And having a son

Moving to a new place
Now married with two sons
She finds the married one and his son and now a daughter
I could of been their mom
A little bit older a little bit wiser
Still in love somebody told her

Now he's single but she's married
Four miscarriages sadly later
Changing different spots, out a baby girl tot

Seven months later a blood clot and died
A bag boy from the store saved my life
Yet woke with her children at her side

Years later divorced again trying to find him
Two sons and his little girl
Remarried he kept in touch through the years

She went to the Lord and he said
"Believe in your heart
Remember 'till death do we part"
The soul mate remarried her twin friend
And kidnapped her son and daughter again
Now he takes care of his and hers

Soon after only to be broken
Again never to be married to him
With her children and the youngest being his
Together her soul mate shared children again
Believing in her heart to find him again
While his child is riding in the wind

WATER ON THE ROCKS

Hey, let's drink water on the rocks
Like Michael J. Fox
Making it through the day putting on his socks
You can drink a whole lot

Take good care of yourself
And bring along someone else
Rush, rush and then slow, slow
Hold and then go

Water on the rocks don't cost a thing
Get up and dance and sing
You can become you and do anything
Look at what life brings
In your own time machine

Water on the rocks
Don't forget your power shoes and socks
Michael J. Fox
We love you a lot

November 23, 2008

MCDONALD'S MAKE A McTURKEY

Make McTurkey and say go ahead and
Gobble with water on the rocks
Lose your fat and still enjoy
A holiday with our Sunday
Year around
Take that first step and gift
With a kiss and have an
A+

By Grandma Jackson and Grandchildren
November 27, 2008

SENIOR CITIZEN JEOPARDY

Just because you're old
And you speak soft and low
I want to show what I remember
As I sit here limber
In my wheelchair I can still think
Do I have to stand to blink
I can still use my hands to write and push buttons
You might need to bring it closer
Or read it louder
But I was born in that year
And I made it here
I do my crossword puzzles all day
With my arthritis and other disease
Nobody really stops by to say Hi
With my children I've survived
Is this the last day I'm alive

I wait for your show each day at seven
Still answer every question
I really enjoy your show
But I guess I am too old
Yet there are days I can stand
Walk over and turn it up a little louder
Just because I'm disabled everybody needs a friend
To help out now and then
Listening and feeling important I'm not just a senior
I was once young and my brain is still somewhat meander
Senior citizen Jeopardy
I can watch you and Wheel of Fortune too

November 19, 2008

WHEEL OF TEXT

Just because we like the same sex
Love can keep us together as we text
I know that word with the missing letter
Our life is getting so much better

Communication is the Q
When I'm not there with U
I don't have to spell it all out
You understand without a doubt

Too much talk drowns me out
With you I can reply
Can wait to get to you and cry
Without you my life is so lonely and dry

I can't wait to hear our sound
In my hand I'm not down
I know U have text again for the date
U are my text mate

Wheel of text
Just because we are the same sex
Put it on the wheel so we can guess
LOL / I still love U / C U later XOXOs

November 19, 2008

THE SHOT THAT TAKES CARE OF YOU

Let's stop the spread
Get far ahead
One shot may prevent it
Before you really get it
Put yourself on your feet
Pull up that sleeve and breathe

The shot that takes care of you
I don't want the swine flu
Washing our hands
Lets us hold hands again, again

Take care of that animal and human
Be that man who walks with a woman
What can we do
Stop the swine flu
We all need to live too
Don't give it to you
Stop the swine flu

I can see you all know what to do

To Take It To Heart Channel 6 News
October 7, 2009

SHRINERS

Shriners takes the pain
Giving love and little gain
They take care of the hole
That's in my heart
Giving my child hope and a new start

So I give my part for others
As my child sits in a chair
Making his way on wheels
Life I know is not fair
But Shriners is here
They really care

I see it in my child's eyes
In the water as he plays
Giving that smile away
For more than one day
We can feel
That Shriners is for real
So give just a little bit here
So my child can make it there

In a big hospital of love
As I take the elevator up above
To the floor
To see my child once more
Give his smile away
For more than one day

Shriners, Shriners
Thank you for taking care of mine
And others that shine

March 3, 2009

THIS IS THE PLACE ODYSSEY

You can go there
Take away your cares
Be who you want to be
Feel comfortable and free
Meet others like me

This is the place Odyssey
For you and me honesty
Games, computers, good talks
Places to go and walk

Understanding what we are about
Ready to scream and shout
Not being kicked out
Knowing what we are about
Feeling each of our beats
Touching the heat
Makes me stop and put it on repeat
Getting to know the people we meet

This is the place Odyssey
Come you'll see honesty
Feel free like me
So cool you'll see

July 23, 2008

THANK GOD FOR FRIDAYS

I used to go in
Now I enjoy their meals
Without high heels at home
The taste is not alone

Thank God for Fridays
Meals on Wheels
Lets us heal
With each meal

We always welcome Fridays into our home
With every bite our wheels move on
Donating all we can
We go hand in hand

Thank God for Fridays
Meals on Wheels
Lets us heal
With each meal

Kids to young adults and now senior citizens
Sharing love is innocent with every cent
We can feel the trust
You gave to us
Thank you so much
Now let's put it in our schools
Having Fridays every day is cool

To TGIF and Meals on Wheels

DELIVER MY TASTE

Call, give my number and name
Now here's my address
Then he takes your order
Soon he's at your door

You deliver my taste
In a box
Smelling so good
With pineapple on it
You dress with a cap
From Domie's pizza

You've never seen my face
Even though I was not in your area
This is the right place
You found me

Deliver my taste
Love all around
Smelling so good
With pineapple on it
You with the cap
Now you have my number
And now you know my name
Next time all I do is call

STAPLES IS THE PLACE

You can copy at Staples
Bring pictures in
Get all you need in one spot
Do a disc
Or just pick up
But when I went in
To put my children's life together
He made all the copies till they were right
He even checked his work twice
Making sure he got every page
No matter how long it took.
Putting them into a binder
Listened to each word as much as he could

So to me he did it with care
So later I could share
With my children
And that's how my books got started
He took time with his heart in the right spot
Here's the book
Now you've got every page
To me that's a whole lot of binder
In a heart of Staples

WALKER

The family place to do your taxes
A gentle man with his
Family by his side
Adding and subtracting
Calling and helping
Giving his time
Helping our peace of mind
To my mom and me you are
Neighbors that we walked into
With more than cash back
We thank you for every cent
A neighbor given every penny

December 7, 2008

I BOUGHT MY FIRST BOOTS AT WALMART

I bought my first boots at Walmart
I pick them out with my grandma
But I hold the bag in my hand
We stop at McDonald's

I put them on
Take them out of the box
A lady noticed me
She said you bought them for yourself
I said no with my grandma
She said you are taking them
Out and putting them on

You pick them out so you bought them
Now keep the box for memories
She nodded and said she would
It's nice to feel you can buy your own
Thing at Walmart at age 8, with a Christmas
Hat on and blond long hair with a smile

SO BEE ... MY HONEY

While I'm buzzing around
Trying to mate with honey
I want you to be
But I'm still kinda of funny
And sticky free with my honey
Anybody but me
So happily the last bee .....
Flower a pollen is you the seed
So bee... my honey
As I fly over you
And land on some dew
Before I buzzzzzz ....
I still feel that
Kinda funny dew
In you
So bee ..... my honey
Don't let me by
I don't just want to buzzzz ....
Stay with me high ....
Doing the buzzzz ... As we fly   bee ....
                                                                           buzzing

March 6, 2009

CLOSEST THING
BEING OVER NEW YORK

Was being in Hollywood
Being picked out of a crowd
Me and some guy about sixteen
We smile and laid down on this
Flat surface and he put hands around me

The man said lights, camera, action
I got a little scared, he held me so close
Everyone stared at us as we began
Superman and Lois Lane
We flew right over the New York Towers
Wind in our hair
We felt light as feathers

I could actually see the
Letter S blue and red
So dynamite
We were out of sight
Yes that was the closest thing
Being over New York with all the lights

WELLS FARGO

Wells Fargo
Got the horses
For you
Take care of your teens
Showing how to manage
Their checking account
And their future
Earn the reward
On your own
Let's take care of our ponies

STATE FARM

State Farm gives you
A pen in your hand to call
In case something goes wrong
Take your time slow down
Take a moment to stop
Give your teen a chance to
Drive safely
State Farm is in her hand
With a pen

CREST IS MY MAIN SQUEEZE

Crest is my main squeeze
Get closer to my side
Hold me please
Open wide brush side to side
Here comes on the shine
Tasting fresh anytime
One on one touching tonight
Gleam in the morning light
Here's the tube squeeze it tight
The clean taste is alright
Lip to touch to teeth is a delight
Gleam again in the morning light

Crest is my main squeeze
Fresh breath come closer now freeze
Holding on to me
Feel the love go free
Here the Crest
Let's not rest
Brush no time to waste
With toothpaste
Crest is my main squeeze
Hold me closer please
Fresh breath come closer now freeze

November 2, 2008

THE CHRISTMAS CATS TALES

Grandma cat chased her own tail
With a bow on the end
She always spices up our lives
Now she's under the tree in the
Neighbor's basket sleeping
Her name is Spice

I put the bow on Cute-Pie's tail
As she drank from the faucet
But she just kept on drinking
As she moved her tail back and forth

Later JC attacked
The talking stuffed bird, now she's
Sitting with her tail wrapped around her
Protecting that bird that says my words

Cinnamon comes over and sits on the sofa
She stares at the tree with the lights lit up
Ready to jump and play
Almost 2-year-old Brooke
Runs under the tree not wanting to be chased
She had that smell
As Cinnamon got ready to jump
She smelled the smell and walked off with a look
And her tail is up in the air

December 24, 2008

THE ALMIGHTY DOLLAR

The almighty dollar
Up went your collar
When you heard the news
It was me not you

You read the number in the newspaper
My favorite number
One day we met
16 our anniversary
and 33 my age
and 7/2/65 my birthday
I had that ticket in my hand
But like a man
You said it's ours
With the jackpot we can
Spend it together
I thought of the rainbow
And you as my treasure
But then you found another
Pleasure and now you
And my money are gone forever
The almighty dollar
Down goes my collar
I still have the ticket
After all it was your dollar

NOT AS DUMB AS I AM BLONDE

Not as dumb as I am blonde
I can take all the curses
As fast as James Bond
Not to miss your service

I got you at the wheel
I'm ready for the kill
When you are out of sight
I made you go through a red light
I'll find you by midnight

Through thick and thin
Somehow I got to win
Hold you again
I want I want end

Not as dumb as I am blonde
As smooth as a fond
With these eyes
You'll get more than a surprise
And soon you will realize
We can have all the
Fun so stop being
On the run

WALGREENS LASTS LONGER

Walgreens lasts longer than battery
It takes less than an hour to get
Beautiful pictures and get your
Medication for good heath
And so much in a store

Give yourself an A plus
And a kiss who gave your first step
And have amazing photozine for 6 bucks
With family and friends
Make someone a star
All year around
With Walgreens

SPEED DATING WITH A CHOCOLATE KISS

You can count me in
Then meet a sexy friend
Get to know another here
In your area to do stuff there
Speed dating with a chocolate kiss
You don't want to miss
To start not to be alone in the dark
Twice a month speed dating
Let's get to know greetings in the park
Then come and get a match
You will find your catch
Then you meet with a chocolate kiss
On a date you don't want to miss
We also have other events
Just become a host or hostess
Join in with the fun
Get together in the sun
Dance by candle light
Just enjoy the night
Love could be like this
Speed dating with a chocolate kiss

July 26, 2008

ARE YOU HERE

Are you here
I'm already there
To have a good time
We serve you like
One of a kind
Hoping you won't
Spend your last dime
Come again to Goodtymes
Dancing out of line
The girls are so fine
Buying a drink they won't mind
In the cage holding on
Pushing strong

Are you here
I'm already there
To have a good time
We serve you like
One of a kind
Before the night's gone
I'm still holding on
Feeling like I belong
Playing our song come on
The bouncer giving
That eye as you walk on by
Maybe you can touch
Later wanting so much

Are you here
I'm already there
The band coming on
Put those feet on the floor
Bending down wanting more
Do that move before I'm gone
Goodtymes we are here

February 22, 2009

I WANT TO BE UNDER
YOUR PURPLE RAIN

I used to know this guy who said
I want to be under your Purple Rain
I wasn't skinny but just a little fat
I had the clothes and could move like that
Baby, play Prince, I'm under her Purple Rain in the light
She's stage dancing with everyone tonight

Just having fun in the rain and sun
I came home and told my mom
She said you're moving up there
With someone who cares

Now I'm getting on a plane
And flying more than five times
Never dancing in line
So many places I've been again

Dance like Janet Jackson and slide like Michael
Hey I really am a Jackson, Hawaii
People would say go girl go, Denver
Off to you know where I'm here

End up in London and Paris, kissed a guy in a carriage
Found love in the Air Force and didn't even join
Yet some guy gave his jacket with the same last name
Danced like Madonna and dressed like Cyndi Lauper
Later on up in Korea I show the Korea girls
What it was like to dance on top of the world
Through our moves we got sloppy and happy
Didn't really speak a word had so much fun

Flew to Japan, Tokyo, Hong Kong
Danced with all the different songs
Came home but not for long
Ended up in Missouri, than Hawaii again
This time to stay for a while anyway
Came back home and took a break
Up in Texas with my real family not some fake

Back at home I started a new life
Traveled some but just around Washington
Meet a man and end up in Kennewick, on the way
Pass through Moses Lake and stay in a tent
Ended up in Spokane, dance country Garth Brooks

People say things just happen. I'm here to say
You can make things happen. Got married 3 times
As you make it through the day
Just believe in yourself and someone will guide you

People say you only live once. I have died twice
And made it through water and snow and ice
Saving people and family lives ending up at home again
When my dad died he told me he wanted to send the
Grandkids to Disneyland. My kids and Mom went
Somehow I ended back in Spokane
Watching our children grow
Back in the ice and snow

Flew a plane and up there in a hot air balloon
Had three kids and miscarried four
Worked even more than before
I'm still on the go

I would do it all again, to say I've been
Just tell me when, gotta get up and do it
Dance to the beat and prove it
Thanks Mom and Dad
Please don't get mad. You showed me how to go
Even when you said No

November 22, 2008

MY BLANKET OF BALLOONS

I gave a blanket to a friend
And told her it has holes in it
She gave me an earlier Christmas gift
She called me and said come get this
Damn blanket

I walked in as she opened it up
A smile came to my face
And a joy to my heart
Seeing all these colorful
      balloons

Lamb Chops was going up
Then Goofy and Daisy
With all kinds of colors
In the purple wind

She can really sew
A stitch of beauty
And remake my blanket
Warm and cuddly

In the midair
Now you're sleeping up there
With a hot air warm balloon

November 28, 2008

CRUMBS OF THOUGHT
WHOLE BREAD INSTEAD

Lay down the crumbs
Pick up the pieces
There's some

I am almost there
Touch your hand
There's the bread
Crumbs of thought
Whole bread instead
Now I have your heart

Please don't let me
Fall apart

WHAT'S YOUR BEST SCORE?

What's your best score?
Golf 72

I got to give my best wing
There are holes everywhere
But I can't see them
They're no trees, yet I'm close

I got 8 holes to go
And this is my best
Score yet
Do you want to bet?

It's all green,
With hill and valley
And sometimes I'm in
The sand
But the pond I really hate

Here's my best
Swing, I'm really close
I made a hole-in-one
And no said 4 score
Now take out the
Flag and give me
That ball
Now I'm in a pond
And I wear a shirt
With my name on it
Golfer 7

WANT A DRINK
NO JUST A COKE

Hey you come here often
You're kind of cute
Oh you're married so

What do you think
Mmm well
Want a drink
No just a coke

I want the real thing
To crush my thirst
Not you who cheat on her
So don't think I'm going
Burst your bubble

Thanks for the coke
It's been real

TALK NEVER SAID A WORD

I never understood till I met her
She couldn't say a word
Yet I listened and she was heard

She started out with her fingers
Then hands and arms
Before I know it
She turned, shake her head
Pull her ear and hair
Give me that look
Wrinkle her nose and smile
I never heard a lie

She could do anything
Play piano, teach her dog
Talk, sing, jet ski, swim,
On drill team, cheerleader,
Dive, and sail to me

Now she has 3 children
A hearing aid she never wears
We both got married on the
Same day about the same
Time and didn't even know it
We laughed that day, we both
Have two boys and one girl
She always says I love you
With one hand

CALL IN THE NEXT 10 MINUTES IT'S FREE

It's free
Call now and a special bonus
You will also receive ... me

So which would you rather have
This or this
Don't wait you just
Can't get it anywhere

Call in the next 10 minutes
It's free
Love, hope, pain, security
What more can you
Ask from me

I'm soft
And delectable too
I even know how to
Cry now don't forget
Like I do

Call in the next 10 minutes
It's free and you'll love me
You know I do you

GINGER MAN

36 D/W/F Brn eyes/Brn hair
Cooking, run, run out of the
Oven as fast as you can
I am the gingerbread woman
Still warm hoping the gingerbread
Man can catch me as
Fast as he can
Pick me up gently not to break and give
Me a smell
Mmm, hold me
Friendly in your hands and I
Might let you have a bite on
The neck if you take it slow
You'll get to have a taste
Then you'll be coming back
For more in
To the ginger for more
Bread kisses

WHERE'S MR. WINKY

Where's Mr. Winky
He makes me turn and
Blink
I miss him yet I am
Awake and I can't think

Where's Mr. Winky
Sometimes he's in the sink
My hands are
In the bubbles again

Now I'm in the
Tub bubbles again

I can see you
In the mirror
Yet it's just me

I can smell you
In the air and sometime see you
Why don't you?
Come around me
And blow me away
Where is Mr. Winky
On my bottle
Make a wish and come
Out of there and then
I'll give you 3 wishes
Children
Bubbles, Mr. Clean

TIC-TAC
I CAN BE VERY FRIENDLY

You got to get to know me
How about a smoke
Would you like a drink
Yes, a coke and the change
What, will I need a tip
Why, so you can sit down
And eat and get to know me

Okay not OK
You seem friendly
68 minutes and 3 seconds later
I got to go
What's wrong
Nothing
I got to go pick up my daughter
Was I too much
No here's the change
What's your number
Will I know so much
And I know myself too
Here

You know you're funny
I'll give you a call
Here's 50 cents
Okay, hello now here's one dollar
Do you know me I wrote the book

GOING BANKRUPT AND STILL PAYING THE BILL

Someone
Gave me another chance
Now I own again more in my hand
A load from that man
Mountain West

From house to house
I end up with a duplex
But only little one of each side
Still I have a home
For my children alone
I need a do it to keep it
Not letting the bills sit
I take that extra step
With Thomas Realty

Every place I go
To keep my family clothed
They still like wearing holes
In their jeans and t-shirts
Yard sale to garage sale
Some give and others I buy
We all help each other to survive
Keep our children alive
The food bank and neighbors

I thank you all
Now I have my taxi van
To put all our friends in
Helping each other again

CHOCOLATE

I'll take you
Back to the chocolate factory
Where the flow of the water
Is chocolate all around
You and NUNU do make
Chocolate lollipops
Now don't eat the blue gum, you will
Blow up like a bubble and
You got to bring yourself
Down before you hit the fan
Mr. Do make
Well for you and you can't
Though we
Are through then we all
Can go home up, up
With this million dollar bar of
Chocolate

JUST HAND OVER THE CHOCOLATE

Just hand over the
Chocolate and no one will get hurt
Leave me alone
I just want dessert
Hugs and kisses all wrapped up
In a bag, not folded up, not a dude
I may be sick
But I am all theirs
I got hugs and kisses
Without you dear

THE Y M C A

The Y M C A
Gives us the moves
That puts us through
The grooves
So you can do it here too
Be in a play with you know who
Me and you

March 15, 2009

WHAT AM I TALKING ABOUT

This is becoming a lot
Of fun
Do you know what I am
Talking about
No that's okay
Neither do the guys
I'm not surprised he lies
I will see it in his eyes

GUYS GET WATER ON THE ROCKS

The guys get water on the rocks
At the last call
The girls get a Virgin C and the guys
Pay five
To keep their love alive
With your sword in the whipped cream
      No cherry
        Just me

GOLD WOMAN

Gold woman attracts
More than just diamonds she's lacking
She escapes in the middle of the night
Gentle she may stop and fight
Only to try to make us right

She's been there
Around the globe everywhere
She steps in not wearing a uniform
Been in that GI guy's jacket and dorm

She walked without an ID
Later on married that guy and flies
Yet she was again misled
Now she's hoping each one alone
Her children she made it safe at home

The gold woman attracts
More than just diamonds she's lacking
She escapes in the middle of the night
Gentle she may stop and fight
Only to try to make us right
The gold woman has done it all tonight

To Me
October 18, 2009

WHISPERING INTO YOUR HEARTS

Health care homes are joyous for
Family and friends all they need is
A touch of your hand and a smile
So come in as often as you care

HOLIDAYS

Holidays, always a place
Where I can get my coffee, gas,
And milk with a card punch
After 15 punches I get
One free milk, yippee …

Design & Typeset Page

This book was designed by Artistic Book and Web Design. It is set in Adobe Garamond type by Artistic Book and Web Design, c/o Artistic Design Service, Inc., and manufactured by Whispering Pine Press International, Inc.

Adobe Garamond

Claude Garamond (c. 1480-1561) worked to develop the Old Face font Garamond. This font has had tremendous influence on the evolution of the typeface developments from the time of its creation to the present. Garamond, or Garamont, is related to the alphabet of Claude Garamond (1480-1561) as well as to the work of Jean Jannon (1580-1635 or 1658), much of which was attributed to Garamond. In comparison to the earlier Italian font forms, Garamond has finer serif and a generally more elegant image. The Garamond of Jean Jannon was introduced at the Paris World's Fair in 1900 as 'Original Garamond', after which many font foundries began to cast similar types. This new interpretation of Garamond, designed by Robert Slimbach, is based on the Original Garamond as a typical Old Face style. However, this font has been expanded to include small caps, expert fonts, and calligraphic caps which were typical of the 15th and 16th centuries.

'Adobe Garamond' is a Trademark of Adobe Systems Incorporated which may be registered in certain jurisdictions.

Alphabetical Index by Title

Acquaintance 186-187
Adorable 57
All I Did Was Wake Her Up 195
Almighty Dollar 344
Aloha 270
Andrew and Fergie 301
Are You Here 348-349
At Ease 196-197
Back to the Future Hits the Present 320-321
Battery 194
Be Not Afraid 184
Be with You 185
Beau of Our Lives 317
Behind a Tree 38
Believe in Your Heart 322-325
Betty Boop 302
Bike Biter 1 45
Billy Ray 287
Black Lace 229
Blazing Sun 205
Blink of an Eye 203
Blue-Eyed Baby Girl 240
Bounce into Your Heart 193
Boxers with Red, Red Kisses 228
Call House Blues 190-192
Call in the Next 10 Minutes, It's Free 358
Carrying under the Wood Now on a Log 285
Cherry Red 83
Chocolate 363
Christmas Cats Tales 343
Clinging on to the Hold That Couldn't Let Go 230-232
Closest Thing Being over New York 339

Coffee, Tea, Come Fly with Me United Airlines	269
Completely Done	26
Could There Be a Reason Why	248
Court in Our White House	267
Crest Is My Main Squeeze	342
Crumbs of Thought, Whole Bread Instead	354
Crunching Down	181
Crystal Ball Inside Me	182
Dancing in My Car	42
Dancing with You Online	121
Days Go By	168
Debbie	180
Deliver My Taste	334
Dimension	110
Do You Love Me	135
Don't Be a Fool Over a Stupid Guy	214
Dorothy and Tin Man	310
Drake and Josh and Sister Megan	312
Dream Time Wasted	226
Drip, Drip, off My Lip	262
Eclipse	141
Empty Cart	305
Every Which Way	179
Fake It, Make It	177
Fall for You	161
Farrah	306
Feel You	58-59
15 Days and Loving Every Minute	204
Final Spin	47
Fingerprints on Your Pants	176
First Her Son, Now Her	318
Fishing for My Medication	241

Five Alive 263
Fly-by-Nighters 46
Flying Colors 304
Forget Me Nots 175
Free from Me 160
Friendship Love 225
From Top to Bottom Headed Back Up 283
Gay Guy Holding My Hand 198
Getting Her Feet Dirty 171
Getting Lost While Finding Him 172
Ginger Man 359
Give Me Your MySpace 215
Go Ahead Catch the Key to My Ride 33
Going Bankrupt and Still Paying the Bill 362
Going through Hell 289
Gold Woman 368
Goodbye to You and I 209
Grandma Trot 227
Guys Get Water on the Rocks 367
He Is Gone 169
He Knew a Friend 170
He Said Where Is She At 224
He Started Out Dumb and Stupid 313
He Touch My Tail 246
Heck with You 90
Help My Friend Don't Take Her 162
Her or Me 166-167
Here's the Book, I've Got the Pages 76
Here's to a Girl That Didn't Get It 165
He's My Man 69
He's Not Yours 266
Hey, Got a Moment 86

High off Life	164
His Eyes Are on His Sunglasses	290
Hitting the 18th Mark	130-131
Hold On!	72-74
Holidays	370
Humpty Became Dummy	309
I Am Check'n	105
I Am Not Going to Cry	102
I Bought My First Boots at Walmart	337
I Did It on My Own	252
I Did It with My Dad Twice	250-251
I Had a Beach McIntyre Too	314-315
I Have No Clue, Do You	159
I Just Met You	156-157
I Know You're Such a Young Toy	223
I Love Your Tone	68
I Try to Tell You	71
I Used to Know	216
I Wanna Slide into You	30
I Want to Be under Your Purple Rain	350-352
I Wanta Touch On	200-201
I Was Sweet till She Got Away	114
I Wasn't Supposed To	238-239
I Will Never Blink	178
I'd Like to Know	92
If You Could Only Understand	148
If You Let Him He Will Hurt You	151
I'm Not a Blond but You I Can Touch	152-153
I'm Sorry	36-37
I'm Sorry I Hung Up	150
I'm the Gingerbread Woman	311
I'm Trying to Get to Heaven	154

I'm Used to Two 155
I'm Your Love, Love Pad 158
In a Doublewide 235
In a Spiderman Wheelchair 142-143
In Midair 29
In My Empty Guitar Case 213
In the Light of Shawn's Eyes 212
Is My Number Really Up 233
It's So Hard to Forgive 256
It's Your Loss You Toss 75
I've Got to Find My Brothers 21
I've Lost You 149
Judy 24
Just Hand Over the Chocolate 364
Just Let Me 293
Just Tell Me When 147
Just Untangled a Bit 44
Kiss Me before You Knew Me 50-51
Kiss 'n Tale 48
Kiss the Sane Away 49
Lady Diana 278
Last Days with My Dad 146
Last Kennedy to Go 271
Laying in Her Bed 137
Let Me Play with It Hard 244
Liar, Liar, His Pants Are on Fire Again 106
Like Thunder 284
Little Leaf 22
Look in the Mirror 56
Look Me in the Eye 136
Looking for Love That Floats Up 140
Lost My Loose Jeans 139

Love and Leave	52-53
Makala, Makala	253
Making Peace with You	144
Math Piece	259
McDonald's Make a McTurkey	327
Melt with You There's Nothing I Wouldn't Do	208
Memoirs of Hell	54
Minutes	55
Mom in My Heart	260-261
Mommy Even Tho	133
Monogamous	247
Morning Still	134
My Ankle Bracket Had a Hold on Me	77
My Blanket of Balloons	353
My Level	103
My Lilly Gets to Me	63
My Oldest Listens to Him	294
My Son Named Beau	291
My Teardrop	128-129
Never on the Left Side Just Closer on the Right	64-65
Nolands	66-67
Not As Dumb As I Am Blonde	345
Not Just Anyone	60
Noticing Me	126-127
Now My Son Can	298
Old News	62
On the Eastside	236
Oprah	308
Our Life Speeds by Me	210-211
Pain from Our Knuckles	132
Parachute	188
Portrait of a Teenager's Dream	202

Pure as Sour Cream 28
Receiving Is Believing 199
Redless 70
Remember First Love 122-123
Remember Michael 280
Rolling Up onto Shore 274-275
Rosie O'Donnell 300
Rubbing in Your Tub 88
Running Down My Side 220-221
Saddle it Up with a Bounce 145
Saxophone Became Sexy Cell Phone 286
Seek Me Don't Hide 34-35
Senior Citizen Jeopardy 328
Sexy Colors Really Matter 268
She Dances on In 303
She Did It First 32
She's Just Too Old 124
She's My Time after Time 288
Shoot the Breeze 27
Shot Down 242
Shot That Takes Care of You 330
Shriners 331
Skin to Skin 217
Smell the Light of the Candle 40
So Bee ... My Honey 338
So Stay 39
So Young 316
Speed Dating with a Chocolate Kiss 347
Spokaneless 319
Staples Is the Place 335
State Farm 341
Stealing More Than the Sheets 43

Still Ends Up Like a Virgin 282
Strawberry Hill 163
Sucking Up the Heat 222
Sugar and Spice, Fire and Ice 118
Tag Me Alive 125
Take That Step 120
Take the Shorts Corner 245
Taking Care of His Own World 189
Talk Never Said a Word 357
Tasting Red Lips 104
Tell Someone Else 119
10 A.M. 206-207
Thank God for Fridays 333
There's No Way I Can Do 117
They're Riding My Shirttail 87
Thinks He's a Singing Rancher 292
This Is the Bus for Me 237
This Is the Place Odyssey 332
3 Magic Words 258
Through Her I See You 23
Tic-Tac, I Can Be Very Friendly 361
Tic-Tac-Toe 82
Time of Passion 79
Time Well Spent 61
Touch My G String 116
Touching the Numbness 115
Trick or Treat 113
Tuck Me In 218-219
Twin Towers 272-273
2 A.M. Kiss at the Light 249
Two Thumbs Up 111
Under the Christmas Lights 138

Up on South Hill	254
W-2 Me	41
Walgreens Lasts Longer	346
Walker	336
Walking on Logs	112
Want a Drink, No Just a Coke	356
Want Some Damn Lovin'	234
Wanta Hold You Online and Off	31
Warm from Your Form	183
Water on the Rocks	326
We Made It on the 4th	108-109
Wells Fargo	340
We've Been Smoking	89
What Am I Talking About	366
What I Can Show You	295
What I Like	107
Whatever	100-101
What's Your Best Score?	355
Wheel of Text	329
When I Was Young	96-97
Where Is Indiana Jones	307
Where's Mr. Winky	360
Whispering into Your Hearts	369
Who Gave You Your First Step	84-85
Who Has a Light	98-99
Who Was That Guy That Gave Me a Warm Hug Online	257
Whoopi Goldberg	299
Why Can't I Fit In	243
Why Not Me	94-95
With the Glove	281
World Keeps on Changing	264-265

Wrong Keys..91
Wrong That Could Have Been Right... 276-277
Y M C A 365
Yellow Rose 93
Yes I May Be a Bum 78
Yes, I'm Going.. 296-297
You Might Find Mr. Right 80-81
You Promised Me a Roll and a Stone..279
You Say You Have a Fiancée 174
Your Life 173
You're Lucky That..255
You're Naked Beneath Me 25

Alphabetical Index by First Line

A gay guy holding my hand . . . *A Gay Guy Holding My Hand* 198

Adrenalin running down my side . . . *Running Down My Side* 220

An old friend wrote me . . . *Andrew and Fergie* 301

Are these the wrong keys . . . *Wrong Keys* 91

Are you here . . . *Are You Here* 348

Are you seeking or just peeking . . . *Wanta Hold You Online and Off* 31

Be not afraid in time . . . *Be Not Afraid* 184

Both hard workers . . . *Getting Her Feet Dirty* 171

Boxers with red, red kisses . . . *Boxers with Red, Red Kisses* 228

Breeze blowing through my hair . . . *The Nolands* 66

But don't take the girl . . . *My Son Named Beau* 291

But I'm touching you . . . *I'm Not a Blond but You I Can Touch* 152

Call, give my number and name . . . *Deliver My Taste* 334

Calling me up . . . *Stealing More Than the Sheets* 43

Could you say those . . . *3 Magic Words* 258

Crest is my main squeeze . . . *Crest Is My Main Squeeze* 342

Crunching down . . . *Crunching Down* 181

Crystal ball inside me . . . *Crystal Ball Inside Me* 182

Dancing with you online . . . *Dancing with You Online* 121

Do you love me . . . *Do You Love Me* 135

Do you really need me . . . *Free from Me* 160

Don't go corner to corner . . . *Take the Shorts Corner* 245

Dorothy met Tin Man and . . . *Dorothy and Tin Man* 310

Drip, drip, off my lip . . . *Drip, Drip, off My Lip* 262

Each one trying to be . . . *The Last Kennedy to Go* 271

Everyone loves her soft voice . . . *All I Did was Wake Her Up* 195

Fall for you . . . *Fall for You* 161

Feeling the music . . . *You Promised Me a Roll and a Stone* 279

Feelings that I never had before . . . *High off Life* 164

15 days and loving every minute of it . . . *15 Days and Loving Every Minute* 204

Fingerprints on your pants . . . *Fingerprints on Your Pants* 176

First we two people . . . *Friendship Love* 225

Fishes in the pond . . . *Strawberry Hill* 163

Fishing for my medication . . . *Fishing for My Medication* 241

Forget me not his name, his face . . . *Forget Me Nots* 175

Getting lost while finding him . . . *Getting Lost While Finding Him* 172

Give me your MySpace . . . *Give Me Your MySpace* 215

Go ahead catch a ride on me . . . *Go Ahead Catch the Key to My Ride* 33

Gold woman attracts . . . *Gold Woman* 368

Got a moment . . . *Hey, Got a Moment* 86

Grandma cat chased her own tail . . . *The Christmas Cats Tales* 343

Half the time . . . *He's Not Yours* 266

He knew a friend that gave her . . . *He Knew a Friend* 170

He made sure of my name . . . *Never on the Left Side Just Closer on the Right* 64

He said I wanta do it . . . *Under the Christmas Lights* 138

He said where is she at . . . *He Said Where Is She At* 224

He was away . . . *I Had a Beach McIntyre Too* 314

He was the only boy . . . *Just Tell Me When* 147

He will never try . . . *Don't Be a Fool Over a Stupid Guy* 214

He's married, he doesn't . . . *If You Let Him He Will Hurt You* 151

Health care homes are joyous for . . . *Whispering into Your Hearts* 369

Hello, can I take you to your seat . . . *Coffee, Tea, Come Fly with Me, United Airlines* 269

Her I am . . . *Making Peace with You* 144

Here I am in a fight . . . *Tell Someone Else* 119

Here I am in my cherry red . . . *Cherry Red* 83

Here I am, There you are . . . *Smell the Light of the Candle* 40

Here I set dressed in nothing but yellow . . . *Kiss 'n Tale* 48

Here I sit with my old guitar . . . *I Try to Tell You* 71

Here is the book of our love . . . *Here's the Book, I've Got the Pages* 76

Here to a girl that didn't get it . . . *Here's to a Girl That Didn't Get It* 165

Hey you come here often . . . *Want a Drink, No Just a Coke* 356

Hey, let's drink water on the rocks . . . *Water on the Rocks* 326

His eyes are on his sunglasses . . . *His Eyes Are on His Sunglasses* 290

Holding him tightly . . . *Love and Leave* 52

Holidays, always a place . . . *Holidays* 370

I am check'n . . . *I Am Check'n* 105

I am not going to cry . . . *I Am Not Going to Cry* 102

I am willing to give . . . *Receiving Is Believing* 199

I bought my first boots at Walmart . . . *I Bought My First Boots at Walmart* 337

I did it on my own . . . *I Did It on My Own* 252

I did it with my dad twice . . . *I Did It with My Dad Twice* 250

I do not lie . . . *Every Which Way* 179

I don't know why I lied . . . *In a Doublewide* 235

I don't play tic-tac-toe anymore . . . *Tic-Tac-Toe* 82

I don't want you to . . . *I'm Sorry* 36

I don't wanta wear red . . . *Redless* 70

I dressed like her when I was in London years ago . . .
   She's My Time after Time 288

I feel pain in here . . . *I've Lost You* 149

I gave a blanket to a friend . . . *My Blanket of Balloons* 353

I give you more than "two thumbs up" . . . *Two Thumbs Up* 111

I have no clue but I hope it's you . . . *I Have No Clue, Do You* 159

I have safety features in the house . . . *You're Luck That* 255

I hear all I feel inside . . . *Clinging on to the Hold That Couldn't Let Go* 230

I just met you . . . *I Just Met You* 156

I know I wasn't supposed to . . . *I Wasn't Supposed To* 238

I know such a young toy . . . *I Know You're Such a Young Toy* 223

I like the morning sun . . . *What I Like* 107

I look around . . . *Eclipse* 141

I look into your eyes . . . *I'd Like to Know* 92

I look into your eyes . . . *Your Life* 173

I looked at your picture today . . . *So Stay* 39

I love you on the eastside . . . *On the Eastside* 236

I love your tone . . . *I Love Your Tone* 68

I made up my mind . . . *Her or Me* 166

I met a man who needed a five . . . *Five Alive* 263

I met this guy who said you need a map . . . *Who Gave
   You Your First Step* 84

I need someone . . . *Not Just Anyone* 60

I never understood till I met her . . . *Talk Never Said a Word* 357

I remember a friend . . . *A Blazing Sun* 205

I remember the look in your eyes . . . *Remember First Love* 122

I saw it in a store . . . *My Ankle Bracket Had a Hold on Me* 77

I see a jealous face . . . *In My Empty Guitar Case* 213

I see you Betty Boop . . . *Betty Boop* 302

I spend everything on you . . . *It's Your Loss You Toss* 75

I used to feel you in the dark . . . *Feel You* 58

I used to go in . . . *Thank God for Fridays* 333

I used to know this girl . . . *I Used to Know* 216

I used to know this guy who said . . . *I Want to Be Under Your Purple Rain* 350

I used to not care for smokers . . . *We've Been Smoking* 89

I used to show him on TV . . . *He Started Out Dumb and Stupid* 313

I used to wear cheap things . . . *He Touch My Tail* 246

I wake up at 10 a.m. with the radio on . . . *10 A.M.* 206

I walked in seeing this family . . . *In a Spiderman Wheelchair* 142

I wanna slide into you . . . *I Wanna Slide into You* 30

I want him dark . . . *Sexy Colors Really Matter* 268

I want to be so true . . . *Monogamous* 247

I want to meet . . . *Take That Step* 120

I wanta touch on . . . *I Wanta Touch On* 200

I wanted her so . . . *She's Just Too Old* 124

I wanted to so bad to see you . . . *Yes, I'm Going* 296

I was always shot down . . . *Shot Down* 242

I was born in 1965 . . . *Noticing Me* 126

I was just a lonely girl . . . *Portrait of a Teenager's Dream* 202

I was just baked at 400 degrees . . . *I'm the Gingerbread Woman* 311

I was sweet till she got away . . . *I Was Sweet till She Got Away* 114

I watch her on TV . . . *Rosie O'Donnell* 300

I watched her life story . . . *Going through Hell* 289

I will never blink . . . *I Will Never Blink*	178
I'll take you . . . *Chocolate*	363
I'm a lot like you but with three on my hands . . . *Billy Ray*	287
I'm laying on a smooth hard desk . . . *W-2 Me*	41
I'm so comfortable . . . *Adorable*	57
I'm sorry I hung up . . . *I'm Sorry I Hung Up*	150
I'm trying to get to heaven . . . *I'm Trying to Get to Heaven*	154
I'm your love, love pad . . . *I'm Your Love, Love Pad*	158
I've been alone for 9 years . . . *Looking for Love That Floats Up*	140
If I could I'd take you back . . . *Judy*	24
If you could only understand . . . *If You Could Only Understand*	148
I'm trying to . . . *Bounce into Your Heart*	193
I'm used to two . . . *I'm Used to Two*	155
Imagine me wearing a lea and you with sunglasses on . . . *Aloha*	270
In the light of Shawn's eyes . . . *In the Light of Shawn's Eyes*	212
In the middle of December . . . *Call House Blues*	190
Is my number really up . . . *Is My Number Really Up*	233
It happened one day . . . *Twin Towers*	272
It hurts so much . . . *Hold On!*	72
It used to be forever . . . *Whatever*	100
It used to be skin to skin . . . *Skin to Skin*	217
It was in March when I . . . *Debbie*	180
It was the month of October . . . *A Blink of an Eye*	203
It's free . . . *Call in the Next 10 Minutes, It's Free*	358
It's in my hands . . . *Let Me Play with It Hard*	244
I've got to find my brothers . . . *I've Got to Find My Brothers*	21
Just because we like the same sex . . . *Wheel of Text*	329

Just because you're old . . . *Senior Citizen Jeopardy*	328
Just hand over the . . . *Just Hand Over the Chocolate*	364
Just tears in my eyes . . . *Dreamtime Wasted*	226
Kiss me and taste the sugar . . . *Sugar and Spice, Fire and Ice*	118
Kiss the pain . . . *Kiss the Sane Away*	49
Laid down the crumbs . . . *Crumbs of Thought Whole Bread Instead*	354
Laying in her bed . . . *Laying in Her Bed*	137
Let's stop the spread . . . *The Shot That Takes Care of You*	330
Like thunder my tears . . . *Like Thunder*	284
Listening to your greeting . . . *Tag Me Alive*	125
Little leaf changing in the sun . . . *Little Leaf*	22
Look at him kissing him . . . *He's My Man*	69
Look at me, look at you . . . *It's So Hard to Forgive*	256
Look at you Humpty . . . *Humpty Became Dummy*	309
Look in the mirror . . . *Look in the Mirror*	56
Look me in the eye . . . *Look Me in the Eye*	136
Looking at each other . . . *Why Not Me*	94
Lost my loose jeans . . . *Lost My Loose Jeans*	139
Make McTurkey and say go ahead and . . . *McDonald's Make a McTurkey*	327
Memoirs of hell . . . *Memoirs of Hell*	54
Michael J. Fox returns . . . *Back to the Future Hits the Present*	320
Michael Jackson's main attraction . . . *Remember Michael*	280
Mommy even tho . . . *Mommy Even Tho*	133
My baby is one horny rider . . . *A Bike Biter 1*	45
My dad gave him his first computer . . . *Now My Son Can*	298
My father changed this world . . . *The Wrong That Could Have Been Right*	276

My mind was at ease with you . . . *At Ease* 196

My mom called me from the hotel . . . *Lady Diana* 278

My oldest listens to him . . . *My Oldest Listens to Him* 294

Needed someone to hold me in midair . . . *In Midair* 29

Not as dumb as I am blonde . . . *Not As Dumb As I Am Blonde* 345

Not feeling the love on my lips . . . *Tasting Red Lips* 104

Not sure of what's in store . . . *She Dances on In* 303

Now I slow down . . . *Dancing in My Car* 42

Now it is your turn . . . *My Level* 103

Oh where, oh where . . . *Mom in My Heart* 260

Okay this is me earth . . . *Shoot the Breeze* 27

Once again . . . *The Final Spin* 47

One by one they pass by . . . *Dimension* 110

One of the three angels . . . *Farrah* 306

Our fleet's in the sand still rolling up on the sand
. . . *Rolling Up onto Shore* 274

Our life speeds by me . . . *Our Life Speeds by Me* 210

Pain from our knuckles . . . *Pain from Our Knuckles* 132

Pure as sour cream . . . *Pure as Sour Cream* 28

Red ruby on positive + . . . *Battery* 194

Remember the night . . . *Completely Done* 26

Right through the back lace . . . *Black Lace* 229

Rubbing in your tub . . . *Rubbing in Your Tub* 88

Saddle it up with a bounce . . . *Saddle It Up with a Bounce* 145

See what I've got . . . *What I Can Show You* 295

Seeing you again . . . *Through Her I See You* 23

Seek me don't hide . . . *Seek Me Don't Hide* 34

7 a.m. open my eyes . . . *Morning Still* 134

She came to us five months ago . . . *Blue-Eyed Baby Girl* 240

She couldn't let go . . . *First Her Son, Now Her* 318

She started out . . . *Still Ends Up Like a Virgin* 282

She took me behind a tree . . . *Behind a Tree* 38

She's sitting there holding a string . . . *Help My Friend Don't Take Her* 162

She's so free at three . . . *My Lilly Gets to Me* 63

Shriners takes the pain . . . *Shriners* 331

So hard to lose . . . *So Young* 316

Someone . . . *Going Bankrupt and Still Paying the Bill* 362

Something exciting . . . *He Is Gone* 169

Sometimes I want to cry . . . *Could There Be a Reason Why* 248

Started going to many meetings . . . *Fake It, Make It* 177

Starting out young . . . *From Top to Bottom Headed Back Up* 283

State Farm gives you . . . *State Farm* 341

Sweet chocolate smile . . . *Whoopi Goldberg* 299

Taking care of his own world . . . *Taking Care of His Own World* 189

Tell me why I can't fit in . . . *Why Can't I Fit In* 243

The almighty dollar . . . *The Almighty Dollar* 344

The court in our white house . . . *The Court in Our White House* 267

The empty cart fills . . . *The Empty Cart* 305

The family place to do your taxes . . . *Walker* 336

The girl that is . . . *Carrying under the Wood Now on a Log* 285

The guys get water on the rocks . . . *Guys Get Water on the Rocks* 367

The heck with you . . . *The Heck with You* 90

The man I gave my voice to . . . *Saxophone Became Sexy Cell Phone* 286

The minutes may pass by . . . *Minutes* 55

The plane is about to crash . . . *Parachute*.. 188

The seed is me . . . *Yellow Rose* 93

The sunshine in my eyes . . . *Be with You* 185

The two half brothers . . . *Drake and Josh and Sister Megan* 312

The world keeps on changing . . . *The World Keeps on Changing*................ 264

The Y M C A . . . *The Y M C A*... 365

There are times when I am warm . . . *Warm from Your Form* 183

There once was a girl who already had love . . . *Believe in Your Heart* 322

There's no way I can do . . . *There's No Way I Can Do* 117

These are the men . . . *Fly-by-Nighters* 46

They're riding my shirttail . . . *They're Riding My Shirttail* 87

Thinks he's a singing rancher . . . *Thinks He's a Singing Rancher*................ 292

36 D/W/F Brn eyes/Brn hair . . . *Ginger Man* 359

This is becoming a lot . . . *What Am I Talking About* 366

This is how my grandma . . . *Grandma Trot* 227

This is the bus for me . . . *This Is the Bus for Me* 237

This one passing flying colors . . . *Flying Colors* 304

Those girls are too young . . . *Kiss Me before You Knew Me* 50

Through the woods over the rocks . . . *Walking on Logs*............................... 112

Time of passion . . . *Time of Passion*.. 79

Time to go on your own . . . *Hitting the 18th Mark* 130

Time to please what you see . . . *Just Let Me* 293

Time well spent . . . *Time Well Spent*.. 61

Touch my G string . . . *Touch My G String*.. 116

Touching the numbness . . . *Touching the Numbness* 115

Trick or treat . . . *Trick or Treat* 113

Tuck me in under the covers . . . *Tuck Me In* 218

2 a.m. kiss at the light . . . *2 A.M. Kiss at the Light* 249

Up on South Hill . . . *Up on South Hill* 254

Waking up with your hand on my skin . . . *The Days Go By* 168

Walgreens lasts longer than battery . . . *Walgreens Lasts Longer* 346

Want some damn lovin' . . . *Want Some Damn Lovin'* 234

Was being in Hollywood . . . *Closest Thing Being Over New York* 339

We sat down . . . *Beau of Our Lives* 317

We were just acquaintances . . . *Acquaintance* 186

Well today is Sunday . . . *My Teardrop* 128

Wells Fargo . . . *Wells Fargo* 340

What's your best score? . . . *What's Your Best Score?* 355

When I was young . . . *When I Was Young* 96

When she walks into the room . . . *Oprah* 308

Where is Indiana Jones . . . *Where is Indiana Jones* 307

Where oh where are you . . . *Makala, Makala* 253

Where's Mr. Winky . . . *Where's Mr. Winky* 360

While I sit here by the window . . . *A Goodbye to You and I* 209

While I'm buzzing around . . . *So Bee ... My Honey* 338

Who has a light . . . *Who Has a Light* 98

Who was that guy . . . *Who Was That Guy That Gave Me a Warm Hug Online* 257

With the glove . . . *With the Glove* 281

Would love to meet him, Tom Hanks . . . *Spokaneless* 319

Years finding Mr. Right . . . *You Might Find Mr. Right* 80

Yes I may be a bum . . . *Yes I May Be a Bum* 78

You adopted us giving love . . . *Last Days with My Dad* 146

You can copy at Staples . . . *Staples Is the Place* 335

You can count me in . . . *Speed Dating with a Chocolate Kiss* 347

You can go there . . . *This Is the Place Odyssey* 332

You do the math . . . *Math Piece* 259

You got to get to know me . . . *Tic-Tac I Can Be Very Friendly* 361

You know I want to belong . . . *Just Untangled a Bit* 44

You know so many times I . . . *Melt with You, There's Nothing I Wouldn't Do* 208

You run away . . . *We Made It on the 4th* 108

You say I'm old news . . . *Old News* 62

You say you have a fiancée . . . *You Say You Have a Fiancée* 174

You say you're taking them . . . *Liar, Liar, His Pants Are on Fire Again* 106

You told me all about her . . . *She Did It First* 32

You're always on the go . . . *Sucking Up the Heat* 222

You're naked beneath me . . . *You're Naked Beneath Me* 25

Reader Feedback Form

Dear Reader,

We are very interested in what our readers think. Please fill in the form below and return it to:

Whispering Pine Press International, Inc.
c/o The World Around Me with Songs and Poetry
507 N. Sullivan Road Suite LL-5, Spokane Valley, WA 99037-8576
Phone: (509) 928-8700 | Fax: (509) 922-9949
Publisher Websites: www.whisperingpinepress.com
www.whisperingpinepressbookstore.com
Blog: www.whisperingpinepressblog.com
Email: sales@whisperingpinepress.com

Name: _____

Address: _____

City, St., Zip: _____

Phone/Fax: (___) _____ | (___) _____

Email: _____

Comments/Suggestions: _____

_____

_____

_____

A great deal of care and attention has been exercised in the creation of this book. Designing a great cookbook that is original, fun, and easy to use has been a job that required many hours of diligence, creativity, and research. Although we strive to make this book completely error free, errors and discrepancies may not be completely excluded. If you come across any errors or discrepancies, please make a note of them and send them to our publishing office. We are constantly updating our manuscripts, eliminating errors, and improving quality.

Please contact us at the address above.

Whispering Pine Press International, Inc.
507 North Sullivan Road Suite LL-5
Spokane Valley, WA 99037-8576 USA
Phone: (509) 928-8700 • Fax: (509) 922-9949
Email: sales@whisperingpinepress.com
Website: www.whisperingpinepressbookstore.com

Shop Online:
www.whisperingpinepressbookstore.com

Fax orders to: (509)922-9949

Gift-wrapping, Autographing, and Inscription
We are proud to offer personal autographing by the author. For a limited time this service is absolutely free! Gift-wrapping is also available for $4.95 per item.

1. Sold To
Name: _____
Street/Route: _____
_____
City: _____
State: _____ Zip: _____
Country: _____
Gift message: _____
_____
Email address: _____
Daytime Phone: (___) ___-____
  *Necessary for verifying orders
Home Phone: (___) ___-____
Fax: (___) ___-____

2. Ship To
☐ Is this a new or corrected address?
☐ Alternative Shipping Address
☐ Mailing Address

Name: _____
Address: _____
_____
City: _____
State: _____ Zip: _____
Country: _____
Email address: _____

3. Items Ordered

ISBN # /Item #	Size	Color	Qty.	Title or Description	Price	Total

4. Method Of Payment

☐ Visa ☐ MasterCard ☐ Discover ☐ American Express
☐ Check/Money Order Please make it payable to Whispering Pine Press International, Inc. (No Cash or COD's)

Expiration Date ___/___
                Month Year
Account Number
☐☐☐☐ ☐☐☐☐ ☐☐☐☐ ☐☐☐☐

Signature_____
              Cardholder's signature
Printed Name_____
           Please print name of cardholder
Address of Cardholder_____
_____

5. Shipping & Handling

Continental US
US Postal Ground: For books please add $4.95 for the first book and $2.95 each for additional books. All non-book items, add 15% of the Subtotal. Please allow 1-4 weeks for delivery.
US Postal Air: Please add $15.00 shipping and handling. Please allow 1-3 days for delivery.

Alaska, Hawaii, and the US Territories
By Ship: Please add 10% shipping and handling (minimum charge $15.00). Please allow 6-12 weeks for delivery.
By Air: Please add 12% shipping and handling (minimum charge $15.00). Please allow 2-6 weeks for delivery.

International
By Ship: Please add 10% shipping and handling (minimum charge $15.00). Please allow 6-12 weeks for delivery.
By Air: Please add 12% shipping and handling (minimum charge $15.00). Please allow 2-6 weeks for delivery.
FedEx Shipments: Add $5.00 to the above airmail charges for overnight delivery.

Subtotal	
Gift wrap $4.95 Each	
For delivery in WA add 8.7% sales tax.	
Shipping See chart at left	
6. Total	

About the Author

Shawn started writing at age 15 at a place called Nolands. She wrote her first song book up in a tree over the water near her home. Her book was filled with empty pages. She wrote about hopes and dreams that she wanted to come true later on in life. She began to travel and see the world but still wrote from time to time. Her life was running here and there, unsure of where she wanted to be.

Her eyes were opened wide when reality set in. Some of her dreams came true as she blew out her candle each year. She always came back home to her family after a long trip to know where she would call it. She would fight to make her life better when she was down and out and then sit down and write about it.

This is her first of many books that she put together and she hopes it will get to high places. Now at age 44 she still writes and takes care of her Mom and her family, trying to get by these days.

www.ingramcontent.com/pod-product-compliance
Lightning Source LLC
Chambersburg PA
CBHW020633230426
43665CB00008B/157